Faith Tried and Triumphant

D. Martyn Lloyd-Jones

BAKER BOOK HOUSE

Grand Rapids, Michigan 49516

CONTENTS

FOREWORD

Dr Lloyd-Jones was not only a great preacher, he was also a great pastor. These sermons reflect the kind of questions he must often have been asked: 'Why does God seem to have deserted the church?' 'Why can society turn its back on God and get away with it?' And if these questions were asked in the fifties, even before the impact of the permissive society, how many more discouraged Christians must there be today.

In the sermons on Habakkuk Dr Lloyd-Jones reminds us that God's judgments may be long delayed, but they are inexorable. Even God's people will be judged for their failures, and need to examine themselves. The theme of judgment is also woven into the theme of Psalm 73 as it dawns on the Psalmist that he had to look beyond the prosperity of the wicked to their ultimate end. But both judgments are tempered with God's mercy. There will be a remnant of Judah, and to those who trust him God gives eternal fellowship with which nothing in this world can compare.

In a world which presses in on the Christian on every side, these books could not be more timely or more encouraging.

Sir Frederick Catherwood

From Fear to Faith

CONTENTS

Introduction

THE MYSTERY OF HISTORICAL PROCESSES

There are many and varied problems in connection with the life of faith. We are never promised in the Bible that our lives as Christian people in this world will be free from difficulty and trial. There is an adversary of our souls who is ever active. His great object is always to discourage us, and if possible to get us even to deny the faith. Various temptations are presented by him to our minds – anything, indeed, that may undermine our faith.

Now one of the main anxieties of the realm of faith today is what we may call 'the problem of history'. It is about the historical situation that so many people now seem to be perplexed. This has not always been the case. Towards the end of the last century, and perhaps until 1914, the main difficulty confronting those who belonged to the faith was not 'the problem of history', but 'the problem of science'. In that period, the attack upon the faith claimed the authority of scientists and their discoveries. The difficulty then seemed to be one of reconciling the teaching of the Bible with the observed facts in nature and the various claims of science.

It is true, of course, that there are still people who are troubled in the same way; but this is not now the main problem. The old conflict between science and religion is really out of date. Scientists themselves have put it out of date by rejecting, for the most part, the materialistic and mechanical notions which governed the popular scientific mind up to the 1930s. In the realm of physics, recent discoveries and theories have put an end to such notions, and we have witnessed in our own time more than one outstanding

3

scientist having to confess that he has been driven to believe in a Mind behind the universe.

It is not the scientific problem, therefore, but the mystery of history which gives anxiety now. That is the problem of problems in this twentieth century. It naturally arises from the events of this period. Our fathers, and to an even greater degree our grandfathers, were not particularly concerned with the problem of history because life was moving in leisurely fashion and, as they believed, inevitably towards a wonderful goal of perfection. The Promised Land was about to be occupied. They just had to go on quietly and they would soon be there. But we in this century have all been shaken to our foundations by the course of events and, in face of these things, many have found their faith sorely tried. They have found it difficult, for example, to account for two devastating world wars, for such events seem incompatible with the biblical teaching concerning the providence of God.

Now it must be stated at once that this is a problem which should never have led anyone to feel unhappy or perplexed. There is really no excuse for this because of the plain teaching of the Bible itself. From one point of view there was never any excuse, either, for being in perplexity about science and religion. But there is still less excuse for anyone to be in trouble over this problem of history, because the Bible deals with it in the clearest possible manner. Why then are people troubled about it?

The main reason, it would seem, is that there are those who use the Bible in a narrow sense, as being exclusively a text book of personal salvation. Many people seem to think that the sole theme of the Bible is that of our personal relationship to God. Of course that is one of the central themes, and we thank God for the salvation provided without which we should be left in hopeless despair. But that is not the only theme of the Bible. Indeed, we can go so far as to say that the Bible puts the question of personal salvation into a larger context. Ultimately the main message of the Bible concerns the condition of the entire world and its destiny; and you and I, as individuals, are a part of that larger whole. That is why it starts with the creation of the world rather than with us. The trouble is that we are inclined to be exclusively concerned with our own personal problem, whereas the Bible starts further back: it puts every problem in the context of this world view.

If we do not realize that the Bible has a particular world view, it is not surprising that the world in its present state makes us despair. But if we read right through the Bible and note its message, instead of just picking out an occasional Psalm, or the Sermon on the Mount, or our favourite Gospel, we shall find it has a profound philosophy of history, and a distinctive world view. It enables us to understand what is happening today and that nothing that occurs in history fails to find a place in the divine programme. The great and noble teaching of the Bible is concerned with the whole question of the world and its destiny.

In the book of the prophet Habakkuk we have a perfect illustration of this. The prophet treats the problem of history in a particularly interesting manner; not as an academic or theoretical philosophy of history, but as the personal perplexity of one man – the prophet himself. He wrote his book to relate his own experience. Here was a man greatly troubled by what was happening. He was anxious to reconcile what he saw with what he believed. The same approach to the question is found elsewhere in the Bible, particularly in the Psalms* and every one of the prophets deals with this same problem of history. But not only are the books of the Old Testament occupied with this problem; the attentive reader will find it running right through the New Testament as well. He will find our Lord giving his pre-view of history, and in the book of Revelation he will meet another fore-view of history and of the relationship of our risen Lord and the Christian church to that history. We should awake to the fact that 'the problem of history' is the great theme of Holy Scripture.

In approaching the study of the book of Habakkuk we may first of all consider the situation confronting the prophet personally. Then we can proceed to deduce certain principles. Thus we shall see that, in essence, everything that caused anxiety to the prophet is exactly what is worrying so many

---

* One of the classical statements is to be found in Psalm 73.

people today as they try to relate all they observe to the teaching of Scripture, especially to the teaching about the being and character of God.

The prophet saw Israel in a very backslidden condition. She had turned away from God and forgotten him. She had given herself over to false gods and other unworthy pursuits. No wonder that he exclaims in acute distress of mind: 'O Lord, how long shall I cry, and thou wilt not hear! even cry out unto thee of violence, and thou wilt not save! Why dost thou shew me iniquity [and he is thinking of his own nation and people] and cause me to behold grievance? for spoiling and violence are before me: and there are [those] that raise up strife and contention. Therefore the law is slacked, and judgment doth never go forth: for the wicked doth compass about the righteous; therefore wrong judgment proceedeth.'

What a terrible picture! Sin, immorality and vice were rampant, while those who were in authority and entrusted with government were slack and indolent. They did not apply the law equitably and honestly. There was lawlessness everywhere; and whenever anyone ventured to remonstrate with the people as the prophet did, those in authority rose up with strife and contention. Serious religious falling away had been followed, as invariably happens, by a general moral and political decline. Such were the alarming conditions which confronted the prophet.

It was a real problem. To start with, he could not understand why God allowed it all. He had been praying to God about it, but God did not seem to answer. Hence his perplexity: 'O Lord, how long shall I cry, and thou wilt not hear! even cry out unto thee of violence, and thou wilt not save!' But, unfortunately for the prophet, this was only the beginning of his troubles. For following his complaint that God had failed to listen to him and to answer his prayers, God did answer him, but in an altogether unexpected way. 'Behold ye among the heathen, and regard, and wonder marvellously: for I will work a work in your days, which ye will not believe, though it be told you. For, lo, I raise up the Chaldeans, that bitter and hasty nation, which shall march through the breadth of the land, to possess the dwellingplaces that are not theirs.' God was virtually saying to the prophet,

'All right! I have been hearing your prayer all the time, and now I tell you what I propose to do. I am going to raise up the Chaldeans.' The Chaldeans were, at that time, a very insignificant people compared with the Assyrians, who were the great contemporaries of Israel. Habakkuk, already perplexed at the fact that God permitted iniquity in his own nation, is now told that he intends to raise up an utterly pagan, godless people to conquer the land and to punish his people. The prophet was almost overwhelmed. This is the problem which we shall study in the following chapters.

OUTLINE
OF THE BOOK OF HABAKKUK

In 1:5–11 God tells the prophet what he is about to do. He reveals the might of Israel's terrible enemy and the devastation which that enemy will leave behind him. He describes the enemy's arrogance and pride in imputing his success to his own god and to his own greatness. In 1:12 – 2:1 we see the way in which the prophet grapples with this problem. The rest of chapter 2 is devoted to God's gracious dealings with Habakkuk, and the way in which he enables the prophet to understand the over-all situation. God gives him a wonderful insight into biblical philosophy and history, and how these things are to be reconciled with his own holiness and greatness, and how everything will eventually be perfectly worked out. Chapter 3 describes the prophet's reaction to all this.

Chapter One

THE STRANGENESS OF GOD'S WAYS
Habakkuk 1:1–11

The message of Habakkuk is sorely needed in these days when so many are perplexed by this problem of history. We begin, therefore, with two statements of fact:

1. God's ways are often mysterious

(a) His inaction

The first thing we discover when we study God's actions is *that he may seem to be strangely silent and inactive in provocative circumstances.* Why is it that God permits certain things to happen? Why is the Christian church what she is today? Look at her history in the twentieth century. Why has God permitted such conditions? Why has he allowed 'modernism' to arise, undermining the faith and even denying its fundamental truths? Why does he not strike these people dead as they utter their blasphemy and their denials of the faith which they are ordained to preach? Why does he allow so many wrong things to be done *even in his name?*

Again, why has not God answered the prayers of his faithful people? We have been praying for revival for decades. Our prayers have been sincere and zealous. We have bemoaned the state of affairs and have cried out to God on account of it. But still nothing seems to happen. Like the prophet Habakkuk many are asking 'How long shall I cry, and thou wilt not hear, even cry out unto thee of violence

9

and thou wilt not save?' But this is not only the problem of
the church as a whole; it is also the question which confronts
so many people personally. There are those who have been
praying about someone who is dear to them for many years,
and God does not seem to answer. They reason within themselves like this: 'Surely it is the will of God that a person
should become a Christian? Well, I have been praying for
him for all these years and nothing seems to happen. Why?
Why is God thus silent?' People are often impatient about
this. Why does he not answer our prayers? How can we
understand a holy God permitting his own church to be as
she is today?

(b) His unexpected providences

A second thing we discover is *that God sometimes gives
unexpected answers to our prayers.* This, more than anything
else, was what really startled Habakkuk. For a long time God
does not seem to answer at all. Then, when he does answer,
what he says is even more mysterious than his apparent failure
to listen to our prayers. Habakkuk was quite clear in his own
mind that the need was for God to chastise the nation and
then send a great revival. But when God replied, 'I am
answering you by raising up the Chaldean army to go right
through and destroy your cities', that was the last thing he
could ever have imagined that God would say. But that is
what God did tell him, and that is what actually took place.

John Newton wrote a poem describing a similar personal
experience. He felt that he wanted something better in his
spiritual life. He cried out for a deeper knowledge of God.
He expected some wonderful vision of him rending the
heavens and coming down to shower blessing into his life.
But instead of this Newton had an experience in which for
months God seemed to have abandoned him to Satan. He
was tempted and tried beyond his comprehension. Yet at last
he *did* come to understand and saw that that was God's way
of answering his prayer. God had allowed him to go down
into the depths to teach him to depend entirely on him. Then,
when Newton had learned his lesson, God brought him out
of his trial.

We all tend to prescribe the answers to our prayers. We

think that God can come in only one way. But Scripture teaches us that God sometimes answers our prayers by allowing things to become much worse before they become better. He may sometimes do the opposite of what we anticipate. He may overwhelm us by confronting us with a Chaldean army. Yet it is a fundamental principle in the life and walk of faith that we must always be prepared for the unexpected when we are dealing with God. I wonder what our fathers would have thought at the beginning of the twentieth century if they could have had a pre-view of the state of the Christian church today. They were unhappy enough about things even then. They were already having meetings for revival and for seeking God. If they could see the church at the present time, they would not believe their eyes. They could never have imagined that spiritually the church could have sunk so low. Yet God has allowed this to happen. It has been an unexpected answer. We must hold on to the hope that he has allowed things to become worse before they finally become better.

(c) His unusual instruments

A third surprising feature of God's ways is *that he sometimes uses strange instruments to correct his church and people.* The Chaldeans, of all people, are the ones whom God is going to raise up to chastise Israel! Such a thing was unthinkable. But here again is a fact which is evident right through Scripture. God, if he so wishes, can use even a godless Chaldean. In the course of history he has used all sorts of strange and unexpected instruments to bring his purposes to pass. This is a very relevant fact today, for it would seem that, according to the Bible, much of what is happening in the world now must be regarded in this light. We may perhaps go further and say positively that Communism, which seems to be feared by so many Christians today, is but an instrument which God is using to deal with his own people.

The importance of all this lies in the fact that, if we do not view these things in the right way, our prayers will be wrongly conceived and wrongly directed. We have to realize the true state of the church, and recognize its iniquity. We must understand that it is possible that the forces which today are most antagonistic to the Christian church are possibly being used by God for his own purpose. The plain teaching of the prophet is that God may use very strange instruments indeed, and sometimes the very last instrument that we would have expected.

2. God's ways are often misunderstood

(a) By careless religious people

God's ways are often strange and perplexing and surprise at what he does is felt by more than one type of person. It is, first of all, a matter of great surprise to the more careless amongst religious people. In Habakkuk 1:5, God refers to the godless in Israel, those who had become careless and slack. 'Behold ye among the heathen, and regard, and wonder marvellously; for I will work a work in your days, which ye will not believe, though it be told you.' Their attitude was: 'Here is that prophet telling us that God is going to use the Chaldeans. As if God could do anything like that! There is no real danger; don't listen to him. These prophets are always alarmists, and threatening us with evil. The very idea that God would raise up a people like the Chaldeans to chastise Israel! The whole thing is impossible!' The trouble with Israel was that they would never believe the prophets. Yet, in fact, God did deal with his people exactly as he said he would.

The attitude we find in Israel is as old as the Flood. God warned the ancient world of judgment through Noah, saying, 'My Spirit shall not always strive with man'. But people scoffed and said that such a thing was monstrous and could not happen. It was the same with Sodom and Gomorrah. Easy-going people could never believe that their cities would be destroyed. They said God would intervene before that happened, and continued in their indolent ways in the hope that God would deliver them without much trouble to themselves. In the time of Habakkuk the attitude was the same. But God *did* raise up the Chaldeans, and Israel was attacked and conquered. The nation was laid low and carried away into captivity.

The most signal illustration of this principle is recorded in

Acts 13 where the apostle Paul quotes the fifth verse of
Habakkuk 1 and applies it to his contemporaries. He declares
in effect: 'No, you will not believe, any more than your
fathers did. But because Israel has not recognized her
Messiah, has even crucified him, and now refuses to believe
his gospel, God is at last going to act in judgment. He is
going to raise up the Roman power to sack and to destroy
your temple, and you yourselves will be cast out among the
nations. I know you will not believe this, for the prophet
Habakkuk has already prophesied it, and you are continuing
to ignore his message.' The year AD 70 inexorably came. The
Roman legions surrounded Jerusalem and destroyed it and
the Jews were cast out among the nations where they remain
until this day. It is true that careless religious people never
believe the prophets. They always say, 'God will never do
such things!' But I am reminding you that God does so act.
God may be using Communism in our time to chastise his
own people and to teach them a lesson. We dare not continue,
therefore, to be smug and indolent, saying it is unthinkable
that God could use such an instrument. We must not allow
ourselves to be lulled into the state of those who dwell at ease
in Zion and who fail to read the signs of the times.

(b) By the world

In the second place, God's ways are very surprising to the
world. 'Then shall his mind change, and he shall pass over,
and offend, imputing this his power unto his god' (Hab.
1:11). The Chaldeans completely failed to realize that they
were being used by God and imputed all their success to their
own god. They thought that they owed their success to their
own military prowess, and boasted of the fact. But God was
soon to demonstrate to them that it was not so, and that as
he had raised them up so he could cast them down. The
world, even more than God's own people, fails to understand
God's ways. Those arrogant powers, which have been used
by God for his own purpose at various times in history, have
always prided themselves on their achievements. The pride of
the modern world in its scientific progress and in its political
systems is typical of this. Because the enemies of the Christian
faith see the church languishing and find themselves coming

into the ascendancy, they impute their success 'unto their own god'. They fail to understand the true meaning of history. Great powers have been raised up and have conquered for a while, but they have always become drunk with their own successes. And suddenly, they in turn have found themselves cast down. The real significance of history never dawns upon them.

(c) By the prophet himself

Lastly, God's ways were baffling even to the prophet himself. But his reaction was a very different one. His question was as to how all this is to be reconciled with the holiness of God. He exclaims, 'O Lord, how long shall I cry, and thou wilt not hear! even cry out unto thee of violence, and thou wilt not save! Why dost thou shew me iniquity, and cause me to behold grievance? for spoiling and violence are before me: and there are [those] that raise up strife and contention.'

It must suffice to establish the following general biblical principles by way of an answer to this problem of history:

1. History is under divine control

'For, lo, I raise up the Chaldeans, that bitter and hasty nation.' God controls not only Israel, but also his enemies, the Chaldeans. Every nation on earth is under the hand of God, for there is no power in this world that is not ultimately controlled by him. Things are not what they appear to be. It seemed to be the astute military prowess of the Chaldeans that had brought them into the ascendancy. But it was not so at all, for God had raised them up. God is the Lord of history. He is seated in the heavens and the nations to him are 'as grasshoppers, as a drop in a bucket, or as the small dust of the balance'. The Bible asserts that God is over all. He started the historical process, he is controlling it, and he is going to end it. We must never lose sight of this crucial fact.

2. History follows a divine plan

Things do not just happen. Events are not just accidental, for there is a definite plan of history and everything has been pre-arranged from the beginning. God who 'sees the end from the beginning' has a purpose in it all, and knows 'the times and the seasons'. He knows when to bless Israel and when not to bless her. Everything is under his hand. It was 'when the fullness of the time was come' that God sent forth his Son. He allowed the great philosophers, with their clarification of thought, to come first. Then emerged the Romans, famous for ordered government, building their roads and spreading their wonderful legal system throughout the world. It was after this that God sent forth his Son. God had planned it all.

There is a purpose in history, and what is now happening in this twentieth century is not accidental. Remembering that the church is at the centre of God's plan, let us never forget the pride and arrogance of the church in the nineteenth century. Behold her sitting back in self-satisfaction, enjoying her so-called cultured sermons and learned ministry, feeling just a little ashamed to mention such things as conversion and the work of the Holy Spirit. Observe the prosperous Victorian comfortably enjoying his worship. Note his faith in science and his readiness to substitute philosophy for revelation. How constantly he denied the very spirit of the New Testament! Yes, the church needed chastisement, and it is not at all difficult to understand this twentieth century when we consider the story of the nineteenth. There is indeed a plan discernible in all these things.

3. History follows a divine timetable

God does not stop to consult us, and everything takes place according to 'the counsel of his own will'. God has his time; he has his own way; and he acts and works accordingly.

4. History is bound up with the divine kingdom

The key to the history of the world is the kingdom of God. The story of the other nations mentioned in the Old Testament is relevant only as it bears upon the destiny of Israel. And ultimately history today is relevant only as it bears upon the history of the Christian church. What really matters in the world is God's kingdom. From the very beginning, since the fall of mankind, God has been at work establishing a new kingdom in the world. It is his own kingdom, and he is calling people out of the world into that kingdom; and everything that happens in the world has relevance to it. It is still only in process of formation, but it will finally reach its perfect consummation. Other events are of importance as they have a bearing upon that event. The problems of today are to be understood only in its light. What God is permitting in the church and in the world today is related to his great purpose for his own church and kingdom.

Let us not therefore be stumbled when we see surprising things happening in the world. Rather let us ask, 'What is the relevance of this event to the kingdom of God?' Or, if strange things are happening to you personally, don't complain, but say, 'What is God teaching me through this? What is there in me that needs to be corrected? Where have I gone wrong and why is God allowing these things?' There is a meaning in them if only we can see it. We need not become bewildered and doubt the love or the justice of God. If God were unkind enough to answer some of our prayers at once, and in our way, we should be very impoverished Christians. Fortunately, God sometimes delays his answer in order to deal with selfishness or things in our lives which should not be there. He is concerned about us, and intends to fit us for a fuller place in his kingdom. We should therefore judge every event in the light of God's great, eternal and glorious purpose.

Chapter Two

THE PROPHET'S PERPLEXITY
Habakkuk 1:12–17
(especially verses 12 and 13)

It is important for the Christian not only to read the newspapers and to understand something of what is happening in
the world, but to understand the significance of events. There
are, in our time, grave dangers confronting the church and,
unless she is careful, like Israel of old she may enter into
political alliances to try to stave off the very thing which God
has ordained. It is essential that the church should not view
things with a political eye, but learn to interpret events spiritually and to understand them in the light of God's instruc-
tions to her. What to the natural person is utterly abhorrent,
and even disastrous, may be the very thing God is using to
chastise us and to restore us to a right relationship to himself.
So we must not jump to hasty conclusions.

1. The importance of right methods of approach

Most of the problems and perplexities of the Christian life
arise from a lack of the right *method* of approach. It is much
more important that we should know the method of approach
than that we should have pat answers to particular problems.
People usually want a clear answer to a specific question, but
the Bible does not always give us what we desire in this
respect. It does, however, teach us a method. We are apt to

panic and to jump to false conclusions when the unexpected happens and when God is dealing with us in a strange and unusual manner. In Psalm 73 we are taught the danger of speaking unadvisedly with our lips. The Psalmist, seeing certain evils, exclaimed, 'Verily I have cleansed my heart in vain, and washed my hands in innocency.' Was there any point, therefore, in being religious? But he suddenly pulled himself up and said, 'If I should speak thus . . . ,' realizing that he had spoken unadvisedly with his lips. He had begun to speak without really thinking.

In every such situation we must discover the right way to act. The problem may come in a personal form; it may come to us nationally; or it may come to us as world citizens in the wider sphere of historical events. So let us analyse carefully this perfect example of the method of approach of which so many are found in the Bible.

2. The method described

(a) Stop to think

The first rule is to think instead of speaking. 'Be swift to hear,' says James, 'slow to speak, slow to wrath' (James 1:19). Our trouble is that we are swift to speak and swift to wrath, but slow to think. According to this prophet, however, the first thing to do is to ponder. Before expressing our reactions we must discipline ourselves to think. It may seem superfluous to emphasize this, yet we all know well that this is where we most often go wrong.

(b) Re-state basic principles

The next rule is that when you start to think you must not begin with your immediate problem. Begin further back. Apply the strategy of the indirect approach. This is a well-known principle in military planning. The real enemy in the last war was Germany, but the Allies began to defeat Germany in North Africa, a strategy of indirect approach. Such an approach is sometimes of vital importance in the spiritual life, especially when we are confronted with a problem such as the one before us. We need to start our thinking further back, and to approach the immediate problem indirectly.

We must first remind ourselves of those things of which we are absolutely certain, things which are entirely beyond doubt. Write them down and say to yourself: 'In this terrible and perplexing situation in which I find myself, here at least is solid ground.' When, walking on moorlands, or over a mountain range, you come to bogs, the only way to negotiate them is to find solid places on which you can place your feet. The way to get across the morasses and the places in which you are liable to sink is to search for footholds. So, in spiritual problems, you must return to eternal and absolute principles. The psychology of this is obvious, for the moment you turn to basic principles, you immediately begin to lose your sense of panic. It is a great thing to reassure your soul with those things that are beyond dispute.

(c) Apply the principles to the problem

Then, having done that, you can take the next step. Put the particular problem into the context of those firm principles which are before you. The fact of the matter is that all problems are capable of solution only if they are put in the right context. The way to interpret a difficult text of Scripture is to consider its context. We often mistake the meaning of a phrase because we take it out of context; but when you put your problem text into its context, the context will generally interpret the text for you. The same is also true of the particular problem that is causing you concern.

(d) If still in doubt, commit the problem to God in faith

That brings us to the final step in this method. If you are *still* not clear about the answer, then just take it to God in prayer and leave it there with him. That is what the prophet did in 1:13. In the preceding verse and in the early part of verse 13, the prophet was clearly still perplexed, so he took the problem to God and left it there.

Once we have the right method we can apply it to any problem: to God's strange dealings with a nation, to problems in the world, or equally to personal difficulties. Whatever the

19

problem, stop to think, lay down the propositions, bring it into that context, and then, if still in trouble, take it to God and leave it there.

Let us follow the prophet as he applies this method to the two major problems that troubled him, that of the apparent weakness and defeat of God, and that of reconciling God's use of the Chaldean army with his holy character.

1. The problem of God's inaction

People were then asking: Why did God allow the Chaldean army to behave as it liked and with such devastating results? Was he helpless in face of that enemy power? People are still asking: Why did God allow the 'higher critics' and other debilitating influences to come in? Why does he tolerate such things? Why doesn't he intervene? Is it because he cannot stop it? Or again, Why does God allow war?

(a) God is eternal

After stating his difficulty the prophet declares, 'Art thou not from everlasting?' (1:12). You see, he is laying down a proposition. He is forgetting for a moment the immediate problem, and asking himself what it was he was sure of about God. The first thing was 'Art thou not from everlasting?' Previously he had just said (1:11) that the Chaldeans, flushed with success, imputed their power to their god; and the moment he said that he began to think, 'Their god – what is their god? Just something they have made themselves. This Bel of theirs is of their own manufacture!' (*cf.* Isaiah 46). And as he thought thus, he reminded himself of something of which he was sure. God is the eternal God, the everlasting God, from everlasting to everlasting. He is not like the gods whom people worship; he is not like the god of the proud Chaldean army; he is God from eternity to eternity, the everlasting God. There is nothing more consoling or reassuring when oppressed by the problems of history, and when wondering what is to happen in the world, than to remember that the God whom we worship is outside the flux of history. He has preceded history; he has created history.

His throne is above the world and outside time. He reigns in eternity, the everlasting God.

(b) God is self-existent

Then he adds something else: 'Art thou not from everlasting, O Lord?', and he uses the great name 'Jehovah'. 'Art thou not from everlasting, O Jehovah?' That name tells us that God is the self-existing One, the eternal I AM. 'Go and tell them,' God had said to Moses, 'that I AM hath sent me unto you.' The name 'I AM that I AM' means 'I am the Absolute, the self-existent One'. Here is a second vital proposition. God is not in any sense dependent upon anything that happens in the world, but he is self-existent within himself. Not only is he *not* dependent upon the world, but he need never have created it had he not willed to do so. The tremendous truth concerning the Trinity is that an eternally self-existent life resides in the God-head – Father, Son and Holy Spirit. Here again is wonderful reassurance: 'I am certain that God is not dependent upon this world but that He is self-existent; He is Lord, He is Jehovah, the great I AM.' The problem begins to fade.

(c) God is holy

The prophet then reminds himself that another absolute in God is his holiness. 'Art thou not from everlasting, O Lord my God, mine Holy One?' He is sure not only of God's eternal existence, not only of his self-existence, and his independence of everything and everybody, but that he is the 'Holy One', utterly, absolutely righteous and holy, 'a consuming fire'. 'God is light and in him is no darkness at all.' And the moment you consider Scriptures like that you are forced to ask, 'Can the Lord of the earth do that which is unrighteous?' Such a thing is unthinkable.

(d) God is almighty

Then follows the prophet's next proposition. He goes on to say, 'O Lord, thou hast ordained them for judgment; and, O mighty God, thou has established them for correction.' So another thing of which he is certain is that God is all-powerful. The word in Hebrew translated 'mighty God' literally means 'a rock', conveying the idea of the strength and the almightiness of God. The God who created the whole world out of nothing, who said, 'Let there be light' and there was light, has absolute power; he has illimitable might. He is 'The Rock'.

(e) God is faithful

There is yet one other proposition which the prophet lays down concerning God, which is in many ways the most important of all with respect to the problem confronting him: 'Art thou not from everlasting, O Lord my God, mine Holy One? we shall not die.' What is the significance of those words: 'My God, mine Holy One, we shall not die'? He is recalling that God is the God of the covenant. Though he is independent and absolute, eternal, mighty, righteous and holy, nevertheless he has condescended to make a covenant with men. He made a covenant with Abraham, to which the prophet is referring here, and he renewed this covenant with Isaac and Jacob. He renewed it again with David. It was this covenant that entitled Israel to turn to God and say, 'My God, mine Holy One.' The prophet remembers that God has said, 'I will be their God and they shall be my people.' For those saintly men, the prophets, and all who had spiritual understanding in Israel, this fact was more significant than anything else. While believing in the eternal attributes of God, they might have been chilled by the thought that such a God might be far away in the heavens and oblivious to their need. But what linked him to them was the knowledge that he was a faithful, covenant-keeping God. God had given his word and he would never break it. The prophet, thinking of the covenant, is able to say, 'My God, mine Holy One'; and so he adds 'we shall not die'. Whatever the Chaldean army might do it could never exterminate Israel, because God had given certain promises to Israel which he could never break.

Having stated his propositions, the prophet now proceeds to bring his problems into the context of those absolute and eternal principles. And this is what he says: 'Thou hast ordained them for judgment . . . thou hast established them for correction.' He reaches his answer to this question about the Chaldeans by reasoning like this: 'God must be raising them up for Israel's benefit; of this I can be absolutely certain. It is not that the Chaldeans have taken the law into their own hands; it is not that God is incapable of restraining them. These things are impossible in view of my propositions. God is just using them for his own purposes ("Thou hast ordained them for judgment; thou hast established them for correction"); and he is carrying out those purposes. I do not understand it fully, but I am quite sure we are not going to be exterminated. This will not be the end of the story of Israel, although, from the description, there are apparently going to be very few of us left, and we are going to be carried into captivity. But a remnant will remain, because the Almighty is still God, and he is using the Chaldeans to do something within the purpose of the covenant. God is not showing weakness. He is not being defeated. God, because he is what he is, is doing this and doing it for his own grand end and object.'

2. The problem of reconciling God's use of the Chaldeans with his holy character

But let us come to the second problem. If God is all-powerful, and if he is in control of events, how can these events be reconciled with his holy character? If we admit the power of God, and see that the Chaldeans are but instruments in his hands, and that their success is not due to their own god, we must still ask how a holy God can allow such things to take place? Habakkuk applies the same method as before.

(a) A holy God hates sin and can do no evil

He starts by saying, 'I am sure of this – "Thou art of purer eyes than to behold evil, and canst not look on iniquity" (1:13). Whatever else I am uncertain of, I know that God cannot look upon evil without hating it. He detests it.' All evil in the world is utterly abhorrent to God because of his purity; he is of purer eyes than to behold evil with complacency. God and evil are eternal opposites. Anything unjust or cruel is far removed from the character of God. There is no question of there being injustice in God. He not only tempts no person, but he cannot be tempted with evil. 'God is light and in him is no darkness at all.'

Having affirmed this, he turns immediately to the perplexing difficulty. 'If this is true of thee, O God,' he says, 'wherefore lookest thou upon them that deal treacherously and holdest thy tongue when the wicked devoureth the man that is more righteous than he?' How could God allow these Chaldeans to do this to his own people? The prophet's own people might be bad, but the Chaldeans were worse. Or, to put it in its modern form, Christians say: 'I am ready to admit the church has been backsliding for years, but the Communists are godless. How can God allow the things which are happening?' Or to apply it more personally, people often protest: 'I admit I am not everything I might be; but so and so is worse, and yet he is prospering.' What is the reply?

(b) Therefore I commit the unsolved problem to God

In this particular paragraph in the prophecy, no answer is given. To the first question about the power of God the prophet received a positive answer. But this problem of the holiness of God is more difficult. After stating his absolutes and bringing his problem into this context, there is still no clear answer. Now in experience it is often like that. You apply the same method which has worked so well in other cases, but there is no immediate answer. What does one do in such a case? Certainly do not rush to conclusions and say, 'Because I do not understand it therefore I wonder whether God is righteous after all.' No! If you still do not understand, after applying the God-given methods, then talk to God about it. We make a mistake when we talk to ourselves and then to other people, and ask, 'Why this? Isn't it strange?' We must do what the prophet did: take the problem to God and leave it with him.

(c) The example of the Son of God

A Christian may be kept in this position for a week, or

24

months, or years. If has often so happened. But leave it with God! This is not only the prophetic method; it was the attitude adopted by the Son of God himself when he was in this world. The problem for him was that of being 'made sin' for mankind's salvation. He knew that his Father could have delivered him out of the hands, not only of the Jews, but of the Romans also. He could have commanded twelve legions of angels and escaped. But if he was to be made sin, and sin was to be punished in his body, it meant that he must be separated from the Father. That was the problem; and the Son of God was faced with the greatest perplexity of his human life on earth. The one thing from which he shrank was separation from the Father. But what did he do? Precisely what the prophet did; he prayed and said, 'O my Father, if it be possible, let this cup pass from me: nevertheless not as I will, but as thou wilt' (Matthew 21:39). 'I do not understand it,' he said in effect, 'but if it is thy way, very well, I am going on.' He took the problem he did not understand to God and left it there. We may say with reverence that the Lord Jesus, though perhaps not fully understanding because he had been made a man, nevertheless went on, confident that God's will is always right, and that a holy God will never command anything that is wrong.

Chapter Three

WAITING FOR GOD'S ANSWER
Habakkuk 2:1–3

1. The attitude of faith

After telling God about his perplexity in Habakkuk 1 the prophet goes on to say, in chapter 2, 'I will stand upon my watch, and set me upon the tower, and will watch to see what he will say unto me, and what I shall answer when I am reproved' (2:1). The last phrase may mean, 'what I shall answer when I am reproved by those who will not like my message,' or 'when I am reproved by God for what I have said', or 'what he will say unto me when he answers my complaint.' But the important consideration is that Habakkuk now realizes that the one thing to do is to wait upon God. It is not enough just to pray, to tell God about our perplexities, and just to cast our burden on the Lord. We must go further and wait upon God.

(a) Commit your problem to God

What does this mean in practice? First, *we must detach ourselves from the problem.* The prophet's words suggest that interpretation by picturing a tower set upon a high elevation which commands a wide view and a grand prospect, such as is used by military observers in order to anticipate the arrival of an enemy. The watchman is far above the plains and the crowds of people, occupying a point of vantage where he can see everything that is happening. 'I will watch to see what he will say unto me.' Now here is one of the most important principles in the psychology of the Christian life, or the understanding of how to fight in the spiritual conflict. Once we have taken a problem to God, we should cease to concern ourselves with it. We should turn our backs upon it and centre our gaze upon God.

Is not this precisely where we go astray? We have a perplexity, and we have applied the prophetic method of laying down postulates and putting the problem in the context of those propositions which we have laid down. But still we do not find satisfaction, and we do not quite know what to do. It may be the problem of what we are to do with our lives; or it may be some situation that is confronting us which involves a difficult decision. Having failed to reach a solution, despite seeking the guidance of the Holy Spirit, there is nothing more to do but to take it to God in prayer. But what so frequently happens is this. We go on our knees and tell God about the thing that is worrying us; we tell him that we cannot solve the difficulty ourselves, that we cannot understand; and we ask him to deal with it and to show us his way. Then the moment we get up from our knees we begin to worry about the problem again.

Now if you do that, you might just as well not have prayed. If you take your problem to God, leave it with God. You have no right to brood over it any longer. In his perplexity, Habakkuk says, 'I am going to get out of this vale of depression; I am going to the watch-tower; I am going up to the heights; I am going to look to God and to God alone' – one of the most important secrets of the Christian life! If you have committed your problem to God and go on thinking about it, it means that your prayers were not genuine. If you told God on your knees that you had reached an impasse, and that you could not solve your problem, and that you were handing it over to him, then leave it with him. Do not go to the first Christian you meet and say, 'You know, I have an awful problem; I don't know what to do.' Don't discuss it. Leave it with God, and go on to the watch-tower. This may not be easy for us. We may have to be almost violent in forcing ourselves to do this. It is none the less essential. We must never allow ourselves to become submerged by a difficulty, to be shut in by the problem. We must come right out of it – 'I will stand upon my watch, and set me upon the tower.' We have to extricate ourselves deliberately, to haul ourselves out of it, as it were, to detach ourselves from it altogether, and then take our stand looking to God – not at the problem.

There are endless illustrations of this important principle in the life of faith in the Scriptures themselves, and in Christian biography. Looking to God means not dealing with the problem yourself, not consulting other people, but depending entirely upon God, and 'waiting' only upon him.

Habakkuk looked at this problem but he could see no light. He was confronted by the fact that God was going to take up those appalling Chaldeans, people altogether worse than his own nation, and was going to use them for his own purpose. He could not understand it, nor reconcile it with the holiness of God. But he could and did take it to God. Having done so, he looked to God and ceased to look at his difficulty. That is the true basis of spiritual peace. That is exactly what Paul meant in Philippians, 'in nothing be anxious' (see Philippians 4:6, 7). It does not matter what the cause is; never let yourself be anxious, and never let yourself be burdened or worn down by care. You have no right to be perturbed; you must never have that anxious care that is not only spiritually crippling but also physically debilitating. Never be anxious but 'in every thing' – it is all-inclusive – 'by prayer and supplication with thanksgiving let your requests be made known unto God.' And then, 'the peace of God, which passeth all understanding, shall keep your hearts and minds through Christ Jesus.' Get up into your watch-tower and just keep looking up to God. Look at nothing else, least of all your problem.

(b) Expect an answer from God

But we must go further and *we must look for the answer*. 'I will watch to see,' says this man. The military watchman's task is to keep his eye on that landscape in front for the slightest indication of movement on the part of the enemy. Habakkuk is looking for the answer. We so often fail because we just pray to God and then forget about it. If we pray to God we must expect answers to our prayers. Do we in fact,

29

after we have prayed, continue to look to God and eagerly await the answer? Are we like this man on his watch-tower, expecting it to come at any moment?

God, of course, may answer in a number of different ways. For instance, you can expect God to answer you as you read his Word, for it is the commonest way of all in which he does this. As you are reading Scripture, suddenly a strange and wonderful light is cast upon your problem. If you say to yourself, 'This is the Word of God through which he speaks to people and I wonder what he has to say to me,' then you are likely to obtain your answer. Watch and wait for it.

Then God sometimes answers directly in our spirits. The prophet said: 'I will watch and see what he will say *in* me' (*cf.* AV margin). God speaks to me by speaking in me. He can so lay something upon the mind that we are certain of the answer. He can impress something upon our spirits in an unmistakable manner. We find ourselves unable to get away from an impression that is on our mind or heart; we try to rid ourselves of it, but back it comes. So does God answer at times.

Then again he sometimes answers our prayers by so providentially ordering our circumstances, and the day-to-day happenings of our lives, that it becomes quite plain what God is saying. God never calls us to do any work without opening the door. He may take a long time, but if God wants us to do some special task he will shut other doors and open that particular one. Our whole life will be directed to that end. This is a common experience of the Christian life. God often allows obstacles to arise, but the way ahead remains clear. God's will is certain. The point is that we must be *looking* for these answers, and ready to recognize them when they come. Having committed my problem to God I must expect God to answer. I should also compare one indication of guidance with another, because if God is always consistent with himself in his dealings with me, I can expect them all to converge.

(c) *Watch and wait for the answer*

The third and last principle illustrated for us is that *we must watch eagerly and persistently*, like this watchman upon his tower. We must believe that God is always true to his word, and that his promises never fail. So, having committed myself and my problem to God, I must persist in looking with an eagerness which knows that God is certain to answer. It is dishonouring to God not to do so. If I believe God is my Father, and that the very hairs of my head are all numbered, and that God is much more concerned about my welfare and my well-being than I am myself; if I believe that God is much more concerned about the honour of his great and holy name than I am, then it is surely dishonouring to God not to look for an answer after I have prayed to him. It is indicative of a serious lack of faith. Nothing so shows the character of our faith as our conduct and attitude after we have prayed. The people of faith not only prayed, but they expected answers. Sometimes, in a panic, we pray to God; then, after the panic is over, we forget all about it. The test of our faith is whether we expect an answer. The prophet stood upon his watch, and set himself upon the tower. Though he could not understand God's actions, he took the problem to God and then looked for an answer.

2. Faith rewarded

Verses 2 and 3 of chapter 2 contain the answer Habakkuk was given. 'Write the vision, and make it plain upon tables, that he may run that readeth it. For the vision is yet for an appointed time, but at the end it shall speak, and not lie: though it tarry, wait for it; because it will surely come, it will not tarry.' This lesson is invaluable. It is an absolute law in the spiritual realm that if we adopt Habakkuk's method, and behave as he behaved, God will always honour his promises. In effect, God said, 'It is all right, Habakkuk, I have heard your prayer, I understand your perplexity. Here is my answer. The Chaldeans whom I am going to raise up to punish Israel will themselves in turn be completely routed and destroyed.' The greatness of the Chaldeans was going to be short-lived. It was God who for a special purpose raised them up, but they took the glory to themselves and became inflated with a sense of their own power. Then God struck, and raised up the Medes and Persians who utterly destroyed

31

the Chaldeans. God told the prophet to write the prophecy very clearly, so that any one reading it could at once understand and run to obey and warn others.

3. The true nature of prophecy

We now come to the general subject of prophecy. In approaching our contemporary problem about the nature of history and the biblical philosophy of history, it is of the first importance to understand the true nature of prophecy. Prophecy occupies a large place in the Bible. There is certainly nothing that will bring greater comfort and consolation to the believer than to understand the nature of prophecy. Prophecy is basic in relation to the teaching of the Bible about God's revelation to mankind. That is why, since the middle of the last century, the attack upon the true Christian faith has generally concentrated on this very subject. Unbelief is always critical of prophecy. The teaching of the Scriptures about the miracles of the Bible is alike pivotal to the whole position of the true evangelical faith. Consequently, rationalism has been very concerned to deny both the scriptural view of prophecy and the miracles of the Bible since these are the supreme manifestations of the supernatural element in history and in the Bible.

(a) It is God's revelation to human beings

Prophecy, then, is declared in the book of Habakkuk to be first of all *something that is revealed by God to mankind.* 'Write the vision, and make it plain.' God revealed to Habakkuk what was going to take place. Rationalists (some of whom call themselves Christian and sometimes even occupy prominent positions in the church) dislike that idea entirely. Their explanation of prophecy is that the Old Testament prophets were simply men with political genius and a particularly clear insight into the situation. They dispute the very idea that God *revealed* things to these men at all. They claim that the prophets were profound political thinkers, great philosophers, or men with intuitive, almost instinctive, insight into affairs. They admit, of course, that the prophets were quite exceptional men, but consider that they simply possessed, as a poet does, particularly clear insight. They saw the inner meaning of what was happening, and wrote what they saw. That, however, is not the teaching of the Bible which makes it clear that the very essence of prophecy is that God took hold of a certain man and gave him a message. God said to Habakkuk, for instance: 'You have brought your problem to me and I am going to give you an answer.' It was a divine revelation.

In 2 Peter 1:20 it clearly states 'that no prophecy of the scripture is of any private interpretation,' which means that it is not something that we think out for ourselves, or divine, or excogitate. It is not something that proceeds from the human mind. Prophecy was the result of holy men speaking as they were moved, or carried along by the Holy Spirit. Now Peter was concerned to comfort Christians who were perplexed, very much as Habakkuk was and as we are today, at what was happening, and he urges them to pay particular attention to the word of prophecy – 'we have also a more sure word of prophecy' (2 Peter 1:19). They should understand what was meant by prophecy. It was not something the Old Testament prophets thought out, but something given them by the Holy Spirit to transmit to others. Prophecy is not private interpretation of events but God revealing truth to mankind.

(b) It is a foretelling of events

A second element contained in prophecy is that of *fore-telling*. The critics, again, object to that. They would define prophecy not as a fore-telling, but only as 'forth-telling', or a form of teaching. Prophecy is, of course, a forth-telling, and a form of teaching, but an essential fact about this form of teaching is that the prophet fore-tells, or predicts, what is going to happen in the future. God told Habakkuk two things long before they came to pass: that he was going to raise up the Chaldeans and that, after they had conquered Israel and were enjoying international supremacy, they were going to be suddenly destroyed. We must insist that such cardinal events were revealed in advance to the prophets whom God raised up from time to time to warn and to reprove Israel.

33

(c) It is certain of fulfilment

There is another element, which is of supreme consolation to the believer: the fulfilment of prophecy is *certain*. 'Write the vision, and make it plain upon tables . . . for the vision is yet for an appointed time.' The events foretold are certain to take place in due course, and in God's time. 'Though it tarry, wait for it.' It may tarry and there may be delay, but nothing can prevent or frustrate the fulfilment. 'It will surely come' said God. The people must be told. What God has promised, he will most certainly perform. There is a tone of complete finality in all Bible prophecy.

(d) It is of exact fulfilment

The last element in prophecy, perhaps the most wonderful of all, is that it is *exact* – 'Write the vision . . . make it plain . . . for the vision is yet for an appointed time, but at the end it shall speak, and not lie.' The time for the fulfilment is fixed. The exact moment is determined by God. It will not be late. This is a very vital principle in connection with prophecy. God not only fore-tells what is going to happen, and reveals it to his servant, and reminds him that it is absolutely certain, but he adds that it will take place at the exact minute appointed, and that it will not be a fraction of a second late.

If we want to keep calm and even joyful in these difficult times in which we are living, it is vital that we should grasp the great principles of divine prophecy. The Old Testament is full of it. Notice how God foretold the flood. A hundred and twenty years passed and nothing seemed to be more unlikely. The people laughed at Noah for expecting it. But at the appointed time it came. So it was in the case of Sodom and Gomorrah. There was a divinely pre-determined moment, and when the time came, God acted. The most striking example is found in the life of Abraham. In the fifteenth chapter of the book of Genesis we find this statement: 'Know of a surety that thy seed shall be a stranger in a land that is not theirs, and shall serve them; and they shall afflict them four hundred years; And also that nation, whom they shall serve, will I judge: and afterward shall they come out with great substance' (verses 13, 14). Later, in Exodus

12:40, 41, we read: 'Now the sojourning of the children of Israel, who dwelt in Egypt, was four hundred and thirty years. And it came to pass at the end of the four hundred and thirty years, even the selfsame day it came to pass, that all the hosts of the Lord went out from the land of Egypt.' How exact! – 'the selfsame day'. So also in Habakkuk's case, there will not be a second's delay. God has fixed 'the appointed time'. Then to Jeremiah it was revealed that his nation was going to be kept in Babylon for exactly seventy years, at the end of which the people would be brought back. It all came to pass. Similarly, Daniel was enabled of God to prophesy with exactness the time of the coming of the Son of God, the Messiah.

So wait upon God. He will certainly send the answer. Everything he has ordained will certainly and most surely come to pass, and at the exact time appointed for it.

For Christian people today, in perplexity with regard to so much that is happening in the church and in the world, this is still the answer of God. Not only is the whole future course of history known to God, and his purpose for the church made plain, but what he has decreed will most certainly come to pass. It may at times be difficult to understand the delay. Yet, 'with God a thousand years are as one day and one day as a thousand years.' Wait for the vision; it is certain, it is sure, it can never fail.

Chapter Four

'THE JUST SHALL LIVE BY FAITH'
Habakkuk 2:4–20
(especially verses 4, 14 and 20)

The import of the message from verse 4 to the end of chapter 2 is that the Chaldeans, who were going to be used as an instrument to chastise Israel, were themselves going to be chastised and finally routed. God was using them temporarily, but their final end was certain. God was going to humble the pride of the Chaldeans and inflict a terrible punishment upon them. The details given in these verses describe the arrogance and the foulness of the Chaldeans with an exactness which is confirmed from secular history. To understand the teaching we must emphasize certain principles clearly taught here.

1. Historical events must be interpreted in the light of God's kingdom

The important thing for us is to see the relevance of all this for ourselves. The case in question is an illustration of a universal principle in God's dealings with mankind. In the present world situation a proper understanding of this principle is especially urgent. If we desire to be at peace within, in spite of what is happening in the world round and about us, the only way to do so is to understand this biblical philosophy of history which explains what is happening in the secular world and its bearing on the church of God. The essential principle is that history can be understood only in terms of God's kingdom – that is, the rule of God in the world as a whole and including the church. All history is being directed by God in order to bring his own purpose with respect to the kingdom to pass. Our object now is to look at this principle in greater detail.

2. Perplexity at current events no new experience

The problem is not a new one. We, in this twentieth century, have been foolish enough to imagine that our problems are exceptional and peculiar. They are not. We are experiencing only what God's people have experienced many a time before. It is well to remember that history repeats itself, and so get rid of that foolish, inflated opinion that we moderns have of ourselves. Our perplexities are by no means new. There are many people today who feel that they cannot be Christians because of the intellectual difficulties raised by the apparent frustration of history. But this problem is as old as mankind itself, and has perplexed people right from the beginning. Modern knowledge and modern events have really little to do with it, so let us first get rid of any pride of intellect. The problem is the same as that of the man who wrote the seventy-third Psalm,* or Habakkuk, or Israel in general. The Epistle to the Hebrews was written specifically to elucidate this problem. 'Here we are,' said the Hebrew Christians, in effect; 'we believed your gospel, we left Judaism and joined the Christian church because of what you told us about Christ and his salvation, and about his coming to establish his kingdom and to reign on the earth. But he has not come: we are being persecuted, and despoiled of our goods, and having a very hard time. What is the answer?'

The Christians to whom Peter wrote were tempted to echo, 'Where is the promise of his coming?' because they were being taunted by the scoffers who said: 'Ah, you believed this gospel and trusted yourself to this Lord Jesus Christ.

---

* Psalm 73:11–14. (See *Faith on Trial*, p. 67ff.)

You have been told that he is coming back to reign; but where is the promise of his coming? Everything seems to be going on as it was!' And it is noteworthy that Peter reminds his leaders that it was an old problem. He said: 'It is all right, don't listen to them. It is exactly what people said before the Flood; it is what they said before the destruction of Sodom and Gomorrah; it is what they have always said.' His answer was: 'One day is with the Lord as a thousand years, and a thousand years as one day. The Lord is not slack concerning his promise, as some men count slackness.' Now that is precisely what Habakkuk says: 'The vision is yet for an appointed time, but at the end it shall speak, and not lie: though it tarry, wait for it; because it will surely come, it will not tarry.'

The historical theme is also the one great theme of the book of the Revelation. However you interpret the book, it is clearly a forecast of history, a pre-view of relevant events through the long course of history until the final consummation. But many interpreters become so obsessed with the symbolism that they miss the main theme. They are so expert in the details that they lose the central truth. They fail to see the wood for the trees. The book of Revelation is primarily a great preview of history, with the Lord Jesus Christ as the One who controls history opening 'the Seals'. It thus contains a message of consolation, not only for first-century Christians, but for Christ's people at all times and in all places.

3. Two possible ways of life: the way of reason and the way of faith

Turning to the passage under consideration, verse 4 reads: 'but the just shall live by his faith.' You will remember that this important statement is quoted several times in the New Testament. Scholars disagree as to the exact translation of the first part of the verse. Either it can be 'His soul which is lifted up is not upright in him' (AV) or, as quoted in Hebrews 10:38, where it is stated that God has no pleasure in the soul of him that draws back (or withdraws himself). The truth stated is that there are only two possible attitudes to life in this world:

that of faith and that of unbelief. Either we view our lives in terms of our belief in God, and the conclusions which we are entitled to draw from that; or our outlook is based upon a rejection of God and the corresponding denials. We may either 'withdraw' ourselves from the way of faith in God, or else we may live by faith in God. The very terms suggest corresponding ways of life. As a person believes so is he. A person's belief determines his conduct. The just, the righteous, shall live by faith; or, in other words, the person who lives by faith is righteous. On the other hand, the person who 'draws back' is unrighteous because he is not living by faith. Here is the great watershed of life, and all of us are on one side of it or the other. Whatever my political or philosophical views may be, they must have this common denominator: either my life is based on faith or it is not. If it is not, it does not much matter what my views may be, or whether I am controlled by political, social, economic, or any other considerations. What matters is whether I am accepting God's rule or not. The famous tenth, eleventh and twelfth chapters of the Epistle to the Hebrews expound and illustrate this truth.

There are two possibilities before each of us as we look out upon the world today and ponder the future course of history. I can observe and meditate upon what I see and then, after reading what military and political experts, statesmen and others write, I can finally turn to my history books. As a result I can make an attempt to draw my own conclusions and form my own opinions. Surely that is why most of us read newspaper articles! We say, 'This writer is an expert; what does he think about it?' There were experts who said there would not be a war in 1939. They claimed to have worked it out, and their considered opinion was that Hitler was unlikely to go to war. Many people accepted this opinion and made their business or other plans accordingly. They were governed by their own observations, and deductions, the application of common sense and a kind of worldly wisdom, or by the political acumen of certain prognosticators.

There is, however, another way of looking at things clearly taught in the Bible. It is not based upon conclusions drawn from the number of military divisions a country has or has not, or whether the time has yet come for some country to strike or not. The Bible simply states that a certain thing will happen! It gives no reason. It just says that it will happen because God says so. That is the case before us as it concerned the Chaldeans. No arguments are given; no careful balancing of the strength of the rival forces; nothing but the bare statement of God to the prophet. And the prophet believes it and acts upon it.

4. The unavoidable necessity of choosing between these alternatives

The lives of all of us are based on one or other of these two attitudes. Either I take the bare Word of God and live by it, or else I do not. If you protest against the idea that prophets can foretell the future, or that miracles and belief in the supernatural are unthinkable in a scientific, sophisticated age like this, you are just withdrawing from the godly way of life. The biblical way is living by faith. 'The just shall live by his faith.' Faith means taking the bare Word of God and acting upon it because it is the Word of God. It means believing what God says simply and solely because he has said it. Those heroes of the faith in Hebrews 11 believed the Word of God simply because God had spoken. They had no other reason for believing it. Why, for example, did Abraham take Isaac and go with him up that mountain? Why was he on the point of sacrificing his son? Simply because God had told him to do so.

But living by faith means even more than that. It means basing the whole of our life upon faith in God. The secret of all those Old Testament characters was that they lived 'as seeing him who is invisible'. They preferred, like Moses, to 'suffer affliction with the people of God than to enjoy the pleasures of sin for a season'. On the one hand, in the court of Egypt, there was worldly wisdom; and on the other, the bare Word of God which had revealed to Moses his purposes for the people to whom he belonged, and the destiny for which he was preparing them. At the time they were slaves and being cruelly treated. Moses had only the bare Word of

God to act upon; but he forsook the court of Pharaoh and, turning his back upon wonderful prospects, went out, like Abraham, forsaking his own country. He went out 'as seeing him who is invisible'. 'The just shall live by faith.' These people staked all on God's Word. They were prepared to suffer for it, and if necessary endure the loss of all things. The same prospect faced many of the early Christians. They were placed in a terrible predicament. They were asked to say 'Caesar is Lord.' But they said, 'We cannot say it because we know that he is not; there is only one Lord, the Lord Jesus Christ!' 'If you do not say Caesar is Lord,' said the authorities, 'you will be thrown to the lions in the arena!' Still they refused to say it. On what grounds? On the grounds of the bare Word of God! They believed that a certain Person had been born into this world in great poverty in Bethlehem, had worked as a carpenter and eventually died upon a cross. But, they also believed that he was the Lord of glory and that he had risen from the dead. And on the strength of that they declared that they would never say that Caesar was Lord. They risked all. They died by faith and in faith.

This is our position as Christians today. The choice is being forced upon us more and more. Is there anyone still foolish enough to bank on this world and what it has to offer? What is the controlling principle in our lives? Is it calculation? Is it worldly wisdom – a shrewd, balanced view based on history and human knowledge? Or is it the Word of God, warning us that this life and this world are only transient, and that both are merely a preparation for the world to come? It does not tell us to turn our backs entirely upon the world, but it does insist that we have the right view of the world. It emphatically states that what really matters is the coming of God's kingdom. We must ask ourselves, as in the presence of God, the simple questions: Is my life based upon the faith principle? Am I submitting myself to the fact that what I read in the Bible is the Word of God and is true? And am I willing to stake everything, my life included, upon this fact? For 'the just shall live by faith'.

5. The absolute certainty of the destruction of evil and the triumph of God

The five woes recorded in this chapter are true not only with respect to the Chaldeans, but as a universal principle in history. Everything that is evil is under the judgment of God. Though the Chaldeans were to be raised up to flourish for a while, the limit of their prosperity was absolutely fixed. The wicked may triumph for a while, they may 'flourish as the green bay tree', but it is not going to last. Their doom is sealed. What perplexes God's people is, Why does God allow it? He allows it for his own purposes, so that the world may stagger under these evil powers, before he suddenly shows his power and manifests his own sovereignty. The principle for us to hold on to is that God is over all. 'The way of the transgressor is hard' whether it be an individual, a nation, or the whole world. Your worldly person may make a fortune by evil business methods and arrive at the top. But see the end of the ungodly! Look at him dying upon his bed; see him buried in a grave, and think of the doom and woe that are his destiny! We should feel sorry for the ungodly that they are fools enough to become drunk with temporal success. Their end is fixed.

And so with nations. Read in your secular history books about the godless imperial nations that have risen, and how they seemed to have the whole world at their feet – Egypt, Babylon, Greece, Rome! But recall their end. During the Christian era the same thing has happened. There was a time when the Turks looked as if they were going to master the whole world; but eventually they fell. Nation after nation has risen only to fall. The time came when the woe pronounced by God was put into effect. We ourselves have lived through an era in which we have seen this very principle in operation. And whatever may be happening in the world today, the principle is still operative. Woe is declared upon the ways of all opposed to God. They are doomed. They may have great temporary success, and we must be prepared for that; they may apparently bestride the universe, but as certainly as their star arose it will go down. The woe, the judgment, the doom

43

of God upon the unrighteous is certain.

Turning to the positive aspect of this truth (verse 14) we read, 'For the earth shall be filled with the knowledge of the glory of the Lord, as the waters cover the sea.' It is not for anyone to attempt to predict what is going to happen in detail but we can be certain of one great fact, namely the *ultimate triumph of God*.

> *Jesus shall reign where'er the sun*
> *Doth his successive journeys run.*
> *His kingdom stretch from shore to shore*
> *Till moons shall wax and wane no more.*

Yes, the heathen may rage, and the people imagine a vain thing, 'Yet have I set my king upon my holy hill of Zion.' Let the enemies of God and his people be rampant; let everything appear as if they are going to exterminate the Christian church! Yet a day is certainly coming when 'at the name of Jesus every knee shall bow, of things in heaven, and things in earth, and things under the earth; and every tongue shall confess that Jesus Christ is Lord to the glory of God the Father'. Certainly the earth shall be filled with the glory of God. The Evil One will be routed and cast into the lake of fire; everything opposed to God will be destroyed, and there will be 'a new heaven and a new earth, wherein dwelleth righteousness'. The city of God will descend, and the just shall enter in. Everything unclean will be shut outside, and God will be all and in all. The ultimate triumph of God is sure.

In the light of all this, what, then, is our final conclusion? 'What profiteth the graven image that the maker thereof hath graven it; the molten image, and a teacher of lies, that the maker of his work trusteth therein, to make dumb idols?' (verse 18). God forbid that we should trust, or commit ourselves to, any power other than God himself, to any idols mankind may set up, even though they be the British Commonwealth of Nations or the United Nations! 'Woe unto him that saith to the wood, Awake; to the dumb stone, Arise, it shall teach! Behold, it is laid over with gold and silver, and there is no breath at all in the midst of it' (verse 19). Put your trust in nothing of man, but in God alone!

'But the Lord is in his holy temple: let all the earth keep silence before him' (verse 20). Not only must the heathen be silent, but Christians must keep silent too. There must be no querying, no questioning, no uncertainty about the goodness and the holiness and the power of God. Do not complainingly ask, 'Why does God allow this?' or 'Why does God do that?' Consider the Word of the Lord to his prophet. Look up to God. Look at the ultimate and the absolute. Then let us put our hands upon our mouths that are so ready to speak foolishly. Let us realize that he is there in the temple of the universe, God over all. Let us silently humble ourselves and bow down before him and worship him. Let us magnify his grace, his might, his power, his goodness, and in quiet peace of heart and mind and soul wait for him.

Chapter Five

HOW TO PRAY
Habakkuk 3:1, 2

1. The character of true prayer

The response to God's foregoing revelation to Habakkuk is
described as a prayer. But it is at the same time a wonderful
piece of poetry, entitled 'A prayer of Habakkuk the prophet
upon Shigionoth'. It was a prayer accompanied with music,
neither mournful, nor joyful, but expressive of profound and
strong emotion. The prophet was undoubtedly moved to the
very depths of his being with conflicting emotions, predomin-
antly those of triumph and victory.

The whole of the chapter is a record of the prophet's prayer.
Prayer is more than petition, and includes praise, thanksgiving, recollection and adoration. The very invoking of
history, as we find the prophet doing here, is often an essential
part of prayer. The great prayers of the Bible are those of
people who reminded God of what he had done in the past.
They based their petitions upon those facts. This entire
chapter, then, is a great prayer.

But the second verse of this chapter is a model of what the
Christian's attitude should always be at a time of trouble or
crisis. Today we are confronted by a world situation which
may well prompt the spiritually minded to think of this book
of Habakkuk. Our problem is again: Why doesn't God intervene? Why does God allow these things? Why are the
ungodly so successful? Why doesn't God come to revive the
church? In face of these things our attitude should be that of
the prophet. Is it so? Was it so even in the dark days of the

last war? Was our response to the so-called days of national prayer the response which we find here, or in the ninth chapter of the book of Daniel? There was, we must admit, a most vital element lacking in the attitude of the Christian church and in the nation at those times. Certain subtle dangers always confront the Christian, as they confronted the prophet Habakkuk. The devil, as 'an angel of light', seeks to take advantage of every perplexity, making us look at the wrong things and so warping our attitude towards God. The attitude which should characterize Christian people in a time of trial and perplexity is seen here.

2. The essential elements in true prayer

(a) Humiliation

We first notice *the self-humbling of the prophet*, or *his attitude of humility*. 'O Lord,' he says, 'I have heard thy speech, and was afraid: O Lord, revive thy work in the midst of the years, in the midst of the years make known; in wrath remember mercy.' There is no longer any arguing with God or questioning his ways as at first. He does not even protest at what God has told him. From intellectual perplexity he has progressed to a position above and beyond it. He does not even appeal to God to reverse the purpose of judgment. There is no request whatsoever that God should hold his hand, or spare Israel. We find, rather, a recognition that what God says he will do is perfectly right; that God is absolutely just, and that the punishment which is going to come upon Israel is well deserved – an attitude of complete submission to the will of God.* There is no attempt to defend Israel or himself, but frank admission of sin and a recognition of the righteousness, holiness and justice of God. 'To us,' he says, 'belongs confusion of face.' Not a vestige of self-righteousness remains, just complete admission of sin and utter submission to the judgment of God upon the nation.

How was Habakkuk brought to such a position? It would seem that it was when he stopped thinking of his own nation,

* *Cf.* Daniel's prayer in Dn. 9.

or of the Chaldeans, and contemplated only the holiness and justice of God against the dark background of sin in the world. Our troubles can nearly all be traced to our persistence in looking at the immediate problems themselves, instead of looking at them in the light of God. So long as Habakkuk was looking at Israel and the Chaldeans, he was troubled. Now he has forgotten Israel as such, and the Chaldeans, and his eyes are on God. He has returned to the realm of spiritual truth – the holiness of God, sin in mankind and in the world – and so he is able to see things in an entirely new light. He is now concerned for the glory of God and for nothing else. He had to stop thinking in terms of the fact that the Chaldeans were worse sinners than the Jews and that yet God was going to use them, perplexing though this problem was. That attitude made him forget the sin of his own nation through concentrating on the sin of others which happened to be greater. As long as he persisted in this attitude he remained in perplexity, unhappy in heart and mind. But the prophet came to the place where he was lifted entirely out of that state, to see only the wonderful vision of the Lord in his holy temple, with sinful mankind and the universe beneath him. The distinction between the Israelites and the Chaldeans became relatively unimportant when things were seen like that. It was no longer possible to be exalted either as an individual or as a nation. When things are seen from a spiritual viewpoint, there can only be an acknowledgment that 'All have sinned and come short of the glory of God', and 'The whole world lieth in the evil one'. The holiness of God and the sin of mankind are the only things that matter.

Herein lies the crux of the situation at the present time. Do we yet see our need of humiliation? Do we see it as members of the Christian church? Do we see it as citizens of the nation? We are confronted by a world situation in which we do not know what is going to happen. Is there to be another war? If our attitude is still one of 'Why does God allow this?', 'What have we done to deserve this?', we have manifestly not learned the lesson Habakkuk learned. We did not truly humble ourselves in the last war or in the first world war. We failed to recognize that the two wars were the inevitable consequence of the godlessness that had been rampant for nearly a hundred years, all because of the pride and arrogance of mankind. Has the Christian church realized that her present condition, and much of her suffering, may be the chastisement of the Lord for the infidelity and apostasy into which the church herself has frequently fallen? For a century the church, speaking generally, has been denying the supernatural and the miraculous, questioning the very deity of Christ and exalting philosophy over revelation. Is the church therefore in a position to complain if she is having a hard time now? Has she humbled herself in sackcloth and ashes? Has she acknowledged and confessed her sin? Then has our nation, the nation that has been so blessed of God, and so used of God, a right to complain? How has she requited the God who has so blessed her? Realizing the godlessness and the departure from spiritual standards that is so true of our country, have we any right to protest? Has the world as a whole any right to complain? In spite of the judgments of God upon us, has there been a humbling? Is there a spirit of repentance? If so, where is it?

It is thoroughly unbiblical and unspiritual to look only at the obviously godless. Christian people, and even leaders, tend to give the impression that there is only one problem – that of Communism. They have fallen into the error into which Habakkuk fell for a while. One hears it said so frequently that 'the Christian church isn't perfect, but look at Communism; the church isn't all she ought to be, but look at *that!*' They therefore see no need for self-humiliation. Many see only one problem, that of the Chaldeans – the Communists – and so long as they are looking at them they are not ready to humble themselves. The lesson learned by the prophet Habakkuk was that it is no longer a question of nationalism or of antagonism to another nation. Nothing else matters except the holiness of God and sin. There is nothing to do but to humble ourselves in the sight of God. Nothing could be more disastrous, or more unbiblical, than for the Christian church to conceive it as her main duty to oppose Communism, much less to be led into such a campaign by the Church of Rome. There is no such thing as unity between the church and the state. These problems must be considered not politically, but spiritually. Our one concern must be with the holiness of God and the sin in mankind – whether found in the church, in the state, or in the world. Whatever may be true of Communists, or of anybody else who is opposed to Christ, my first question must be: What about myself? Does the fact that there are others worse than I am mean that I am all right? Not as Daniel or Habakkuk saw it! All of us, like Habakkuk, must confess to God: 'We have sinned against thee, and we have no right to plead any mitigation of the sentence in thy holy presence.' Such a self-humbling in the presence of God is desperately needed.

(b) Adoration

But there is a second element in the prayer, that of *adoration*. 'O Lord, I have heard thy speech, and was afraid.' 'Was afraid' does not mean that Habakkuk was afraid of the things that were going to happen as revealed to him by God. There was no fear of the suffering that was coming. The expression suggests awe in the presence of such a great God, worshipful adoration and wonder of God and his ways. God had told him something about his historical plan, and the prophet, meditating upon the fact that God is in his holy temple and the world beneath his feet, stood in amazement and reverential awe. When he realized the almightiness and the holiness of God he said, 'I was afraid'. What is described in the Epistle to the Hebrews as an attitude of 'reverence and godly fear' is an attitude strangely lacking amongst us, even among evangelicals. There is far too much easy familiarity with the Most High. Thank God, we can come into his presence with holy boldness through the blood of Christ. But that should never lessen our reverence and godly fear. God's ancient people, especially the most spiritual among them, were so conscious of the holiness and the greatness of God that they trembled even to use his name. The sanctity and the holiness and the almightiness of God was something which made them almost speechless – 'I was afraid'. We should approach him 'with reverence and godly fear, for our God is a consuming fire'.

This is essential for an understanding of the times in which we live. We must learn to see God in his holy temple above the flux of history, and above the changing scenes of time. In God's presence the one thing that stands out is the holy

51

nature of God and our own sin. We humble ourselves and with reverence adore him.

(c) Petition

Lastly, we come to *the element of petition*. 'In nothing be anxious,' says the apostle Paul, 'but in every thing by prayer and supplication with thanksgiving let your requests be made known unto God'. True prayer always includes these same three elements: humiliation, adoration, petition. What is the petition in Habakkuk's case? Not a petition for deliverance and ease, nor a petition that God will spare, nor that there may be no war against the Chaldeans; not that there may be no suffering, no sacking of Jerusalem, and no razing the temple to the ground. There was no such petition because he had come to see that these events were both inevitable, and well-deserved, He does not pray that God would change his plan. The prophet's one burden now was a concern for God's cause, God's work, and God's purpose in his own nation and in the entire world. His one desire was that things should be right. He had come to the position in which, in effect, he said, 'Whatever I and my countrymen may have to suffer is of no concern so long as *thy work* is revived and kept pure.' His one great plea was that God would revive his work in the midst of the years – 'O Lord, revive thy work in the midst of the years, in the midst of the years make known.'

The expression, 'in the midst of the years' must surely mean, 'while these terrible things prophesied are actually taking place amongst us' or 'in the midst of the years of suffering and calamity which thou hast foretold, even then, O Lord, revive thy work'. This is a most appropriate prayer for the church of today. If we are not more concerned for the purity of the church than with the fact that we are faced by the possibility of another war, that is a serious reflection upon our Christianity. What is it that is chiefly worrying us as Christians? Is it events in the world around us? Or is it the name and the glory of our Almighty God, the health and the condition of his church, the prosperity and the future of his cause among men? For Habakkuk there was only one concern. In spite of what he knew was going to happen, he prayed for a reviving of God's cause in Israel.

The Hebrew word 'revive' has the primary meaning of 'preserve', or 'keep alive'. Habakkuk's great fear was that the church was going to be destroyed altogether, so he prayed 'Preserve it, O God, keep it alive, don't let it be overwhelmed'. But to revive means not only to keep alive or to preserve, but also to purify and correct, to get rid of the evil. This is always an essential accompaniment whenever God revives. In the history of every revival, we read of God purifying, getting rid of the sin, the dross, and the things that were hindering his cause.

There is a further idea also that, while the church is being preserved, purified and corrected, she is at the same time being prepared for deliverance. The prophet looks at the approaching calamity and says: 'O Lord, even while we are being chastised, prepare us for the deliverance that is to come. Make all thy people worthy of thy blessings.' 'Remember thy work,' he seems to say, 'and make it as it is meant to be; let the church function as it ought to function'. This prayer, like Daniel's also, was very literally answered even when they were in captivity in Babylon and in the hands of the Chaldeans. God answered the prayer for reviving through chastisement, and even during the time that chastisement was being administered.

Habakkuk's final appeal is most touching – 'In wrath,' he says, 'remember mercy.' Matthew Henry points out that he does not turn to God and say, 'O Lord, I do see that this punishment was necessary, but I would remind thee that we have tried to be good and that there have been worse times in our history.' He does not ask God to remember them because of any of their merits, but he asks him in wrath to remember mercy. By 'wrath' is meant God's perfect righteousness and justice. The only thing he does is to remind God of his own nature, and of that other aspect of his holy being – his mercy. He seems to say: 'Temper wrath with mercy. We have nothing to say but to ask that thou shouldest act like thyself, and in the midst of wrath shouldest have pity upon us.'

Here we have the model prayer for just such a time as this. In all our 'national days of prayer' during the last war there seemed to be an assumption that *we* were all right, and all

53

we had to do was to ask God to defeat our enemies who alone were all wrong. No place seemed to be given for any real humiliation, or confession of sin, or bemoaning of our utter sinfulness and departure from God. The message of this book is that until we truly humble ourselves, forgetting other people and those who are worse than we are, until we see ourselves as we are in the sight of God, and confess our sins and commit ourselves into his Almighty hands, we have no right to look for peace and happiness. Until the world learns these mighty lessons from the Word of God there is no hope for it. There will be wars and further wars. God grant us grace to accept this message from the Bible, and to learn to see things not politically but spiritually.

There is a personal application of this principle. We must face our personal situation in the same way by asking: Is there something in my life that is meriting the chastisement of God? Have I been what I ought to be? Let us examine ourselves and humble ourselves under the mighty hand of God, and be concerned chiefly about the state of our souls. The trouble is that we always look at the situation and the problem instead of trying to discover whether there is anything in our souls that leads God so to deal with us. The moment I become really concerned about the state of my soul, instead of my affliction, I am on the high road to God's blessing. The Epistle to the Hebrews declares that chastisement is a proof that we are God's children. 'Whom the Lord loveth, he chasteneth.' If we do not know what chastisement means we ought to be alarmed because, if we are children of God, he is concerned about us and is bringing us to perfection. If we do not listen to his appeals he will bring us by another way to his desired end. 'Whom the Lord loveth he chasteneth and scourgeth every son whom he receiveth.' When things are apparently going against us, the thing to do is not to look at the situation and ask questions, but to look at ourselves and say: 'What of my soul? What is God saying to me and doing to me? What is it in me that is meriting all this?' After examining ourselves, and humbling ourselves, we should place ourselves in the hands of God and say 'Thy way, not mine, O Lord, however hard it be. My one concern is that my soul should be right. I ask only that in wrath thou shouldest remember mercy. But, above all, go on with thy work that my soul may be revived, and that I may become well-pleasing in thy sight'.

That was the attitude of Habakkuk. That has been the attitude of all God's true prophets. That is always the attitude of the church at every time of true reviving and spiritual awakening. And that is the only right, biblical and spiritual attitude for the church and individual Christians at this present hour. We should think less about the menace of Communism or anything else that threatens the church, and be more concerned about the health and purity of the church: most of all about the holiness of God and the sin of mankind.

Chapter Six

HOW TO REJOICE IN TRIBULATIONS
Habakkuk 3:3–19

1. Faith and fear

'When I heard, my belly trembled; my lips quivered at the voice: rottenness entered into my bones, and I trembled in myself, that I might rest in the day of trouble: when he cometh up unto the people, he will invade them with his troops' (verse 16). The prophet no longer has any theological or philosophical problems. He sees everything perfectly clearly; but he is only human after all, and seeing the judgments that are coming, he is filled with fear. How can he find inward peace when all these things are impending? How will he stand up to them? It is great comfort to know that these mighty prophets of God were but human beings like ourselves and subject to the same frailties as ourselves. We are inclined to think of them as people apart because of the greatness of their understanding. But if we do so we shall derive much less benefit from a consideration of their writings. Here, then, we get a glimpse into this man's character. He is honest enough to tell us that when he heard what God had to tell him he trembled like a leaf. Our Lord recognized this same human frailty when he said, 'the spirit indeed is willing but the flesh is weak.' We should thank God for this distinction between lack of faith and the weakness of the flesh. God's greatest heroes of faith often quailed physically at certain prospects which confronted them. To see the truth and understand the doctrines is most important, but despite this clear understanding we may still tremble physically. To do so under certain terrible conditions does not necessarily mean that you have no faith, though the devil will try to persuade you so. If ever you are so tempted, remember Habakkuk! Habakkuk understood perfectly, yet he trembled like a leaf through the sheer weakness of his flesh.

2. God's provision for the fearful prophet

(a) The example of God's servants

God 'knoweth our frame; he remembereth that we are dust'. He understands our human weakness, and has made wonderful provision for us. First of all, he graciously tells us that even his greatest servants have known something of physical fear combined with faith in his Word. We have seen that this was so with Habakkuk. But even Abraham, the man of great faith, knew at times what it was to be weak in the flesh. David, too, admitted that the flesh seemed to be failing him in spite of his faith. Jeremiah, like Habakkuk, was given a dark prophecy to deliver, and felt at times that he could not face the ordeal. The message was so terrible that, though in spirit he was ready to give it, his flesh naturally shrank from it. We get a glimpse of John the Baptist languishing in the prison, tired, suffering physically, and with these conditions reacting upon his spirit. We observe it even in the case of the mighty St Paul. He tells us in the second Epistle to the Corinthians that his flesh had no rest. He was 'troubled on every side; without were fightings, within were fears'. And when he preached for the first time in Corinth he did so 'in weakness, fear and much trembling'. Such examples assure us that God understands us, and in his mercy will show us a way out of our difficulties.

(b) The gift of joy, not self-control

Now what can someone do in such a state of human weakness? What was there to sustain someone like this when the Chaldeans arrived and began to destroy the city? What was it that sustained the faithful remnant of the people of God when everything apparently was lost? It was not merely resignation or saying: 'Well, there is no use crying over spilt milk, or getting alarmed and excited, because we cannot do anything about it.' Nor was it just applying the principle of psychological detachment. It was not taking oneself in hand and saying: 'The best thing is not to think about it! Go to the pictures, read novels and don't think!' – a sort of escapism. Neither was it an attempt at being courageous. There is here no exhortation to courage. There is something infinitely greater than just making a mighty effort of the will and saying: 'I am not going to whimper or cry, I am going to be a man.' Habakkuk admits that his 'belly trembled', his lips quivered at the voice, and rottenness entered into his bones.

Now 'psychological' treatment differs greatly from the scriptural method. It is often sheer cruelty to a person who is in a state of uncontrolled fear to say to him, 'Pull yourself together'. If he could he would, and the trembling would stop. But the prophet is in a state in which he is unable to control his physical reactions. He cannot stop himself trembling, try as he will. The methods which the world offers at such a time are effective only for certain people, and at a stage when their help is hardly necessary. They are of no value when a person is in this stage of utter physical alarm.

Instead of mere resignation, or plucking up one's courage, the Scripture shows that it is possible even under such conditions to be in a state of actual rejoicing: 'Although the fig tree shall not blossom, neither shall fruit be in the vines; the labour of the olive shall fail, and the fields shall yield no meat; the flock shall be cut off from the fold, and there shall be no herd in the stalls: yet I will rejoice in the Lord, I will joy in the God of my salvation' (verses 17, 18). The Christian claims nothing less than that. Your worldly person may, if he is in a physically good condition, school himself to a state of resignation. He may put on a courageous air as many did during the last war, and as many will continue to do. And that as far as it goes is a commendable spirit. But, in contrast to that, the Christian is assured that though he may be a person who is physically disposed to be thoroughly alarmed, he may experience not only strength but positive joy in the midst of danger. He may 'rejoice in tribulation' and be triumphant in the midst of the worst circumstances. That is the challenge of the Christian position. Herein we as Christians are to differ from the world. When hell is let loose, and the worst comes to the worst, we are to do more than 'put up with it' or 'be steady'. We are to know a holy joy and manifest a spirit of rejoicing. We are to be 'more than conquerors', instead of merely exercising self-control with the aid of an iron will. We are to rejoice in the Lord and to joy in the God of our salvation. Such a time is a test for our Christian profession. If we are not then more than conquerors we are failing as Christians.

(c) The encouragement of history

Now, what is it that makes this possible? The prophet finds his consolation in a right and Christian interpretation of history, to which reference has earlier been made. Whenever, in the Psalms, the writer faces situations such as we are envisaging, he invariably looks back at the history of God's dealings with people and thus finds himself praising God and rejoicing. The prophet likewise here reminds himself of certain of the great facts in the long story of the children of Israel, concentrating especially on the deliverance of Israel from the bondage in Egypt, their passage through the Red Sea, their journey through the wilderness, the defeat of their enemies and their occupation of Canaan.

We too must learn to employ this method. It may be that this will be the only thing that will hold us in the days that lie ahead. As we look out upon the world today is there any cause for rejoicing but this? Whatever may come, if we should ever find ourselves in the fearful state so graphically described by the prophet, the thing to do will be to look back at history.

First, we must *concentrate upon the facts* and realize that they are facts. The prophet goes into great detail in telling us of the things that God had done – how he had divided the Red Sea, halted the sun, and controlled the very elements. There is no question that the facts of the biblical record need to be emphasized above everything else in these days. There are those who tell us that what is needed is a return to biblical theology and a new understanding of the teaching of the Bible. They talk a great deal about the wonderful re-discovery in recent years of the essential message of the Bible. This is the emphasis of what is known as the 'Neo-orthodoxy'. Most of them use the term 'myth' to describe many of the historical facts, and they say that the actual history is really not important in itself. The events recorded do not ultimately matter. What matters is the *teaching* that is enshrined in the supposed facts. They suggest that the historical details of the Old Testament are not of the first importance, and that it is not really essential for you to believe the facts. What is important is to believe the message which is presented in that form. Hence, many of them do not believe that the children of Israel did literally walk through the Red Sea. They say that it is scientifically impossible. However, they agree that there is an important principle enshrined in the story, and the main thing is to understand that principle. The current term 'myth' implies that the 'shell' of history is unimportant; it is the 'kernel' of truth that matters. The actual facts presented may not be true in themselves but what they represent is true.

Now if that view is true I have no consolation at all. If God did not actually do the things recorded in the Old Testament for Israel, then the whole Bible may be just a piece of psychology meant to keep me happy. The Bible, however, plainly shows that my comfort and consolation lie in facts – the fact that God has done certain things and that they have literally happened. The God in whom I believe is the God who could and *did* divide the Red Sea and the river Jordan. In reminding himself and us of these things, Habakkuk is not just comforting himself by playing with ideas; he is speaking of the things that God has *actually done*. The Christian faith is solidly based upon facts, not ideas. And if the facts recorded in the Bible are not true, then I have no hope and no comfort. For we are not saved by ideas; but by facts, by events. The Christian faith differs from all other religions in that its doctrines are based upon facts. Buddhism, Hinduism and other faiths rest upon theories and ideas. In the Christian faith alone we are dealing with facts. We must reject as from the devil this modern theory about 'myth'. The facts believed and accepted as such by our Lord are absolutely essential.

Having established the facts, we must reckon on *the greatness of God's power*. The prophet reminds himself of the miracles that God worked in Egypt: 'His brightness was as the light; he had horns coming out of his hand: and there was the hiding of his power. Before him went the pestilence' (verses 4, 5). Then he speaks of the dividing of the Red Sea: 'Was the Lord displeased against the rivers? was thine anger against the rivers? was thy wrath against the sea, that thou didst ride upon thine horses and thy chariots of salvation?' (verse 8). It is important to accept the fact that Pharaoh and his hosts were literally drowned in the sea. The story is not a mere allegory of deliverance but an event that actually happened and by which God displayed his power.

There follow references to Mount Sinai, to the dividing of the waters of Jordan, and then there is that striking phrase, 'The sun and moon stood still in their habitation' (verse 11). God arrested the sun in order that the children of Israel might triumph. The God in whom we believe can act, and does act, how and when it pleases him. Habakkuk is meditating upon the greatness and the power of God and the miraculous element in God's dealing with his people. If the substance of these miracles is not true, where is our comfort and consolation? The facts are important because they reveal the greatness and the power of God, and the miraculous element in God's dealing with his people.

The third truth is that the God with whom we have to do is *a God who is true to his word and keeps his promises.* 'Thy bow was made quite naked, according to the oaths of the tribes, even thy word. Thou didst cleave the earth with rivers' (verse 9). The prophet in reminding himself of the facts and of the power of God, is also assuring himself that, in these events, God was but keeping his word and fulfilling the oath given to Abraham, and repeated to Isaac and Jacob. God had said they were his people and that he had certain purposes for them, and so, though they seemed to be overwhelmed in Egypt, he brought them out and sustained them in all their troubles.

We now see clearly the divinely provided way to deal with the fear which we cannot control ourselves. We look back and think about God. When the prophet did this, he began to feel better. He forgot his nerves and, in contemplation of the mighty, miracle-working God, he was so filled with wonder that he began to rejoice. He then felt he could face whatever might come. In spite of everything he could rejoice in the Lord, and joy in the God of his salvation. Such a God, he knew, would not forget him, and such a God would certainly bring him through.

3. God's multiplied provision for his fearful church

These are the facts which the prophet Habakkuk remembered for his own consolation. But we today are in a still more wonderful position than Habakkuk. We can add to the history, we can supplement the facts adduced by the prophet. We are in a position to see how everything that God revealed to him was literally fulfilled. The Chaldeans were indeed raised up; they did destroy the Israelites; the Israelites were carried away captive into Babylon. But, in due time, God turned upon the Chaldeans and destroyed them, and brought back the remnant of Israel to Jerusalem. The city was re-established and the temple was rebuilt.

We can go further. We can look at the facts of the mighty salvation that God has worked out in Christ. We may rejoice especially in the fact of the resurrection. If ever a situation seemed absolutely hopeless it was when the Son of God was crucified on a tree and buried in a grave. The disciples were dejected, for indeed the end seemed to have come. But God acted in the miracle of the resurrection. He showed that he was still God and that, with him, nothing was impossible. The resurrection of Jesus Christ is not an idea; but a literal, historical fact. If it is not, there is no gospel. We do not believe merely in some persistence of life beyond the grave. We do not merely say that Jesus still lives. We declare that he literally rose from the grave in the body. Everything depends on the truth of this.

Consider some further facts. The Jews persecuted God's people cruelly, and were warned that if they persisted in so doing they would be finally destroyed. They had been warned in the Old Testament; they were warned again by John the Baptist and by Christ himself. When they persisted in wrong-doing, God destroyed their city in AD 70. The temple was cast down and the people were scattered among the nations, where they still remain. The events of AD 70 must never be forgotten. Never forget, either, what happened to the Roman Empire which persecuted the Christian church and tried to destroy her. But it had been clearly revealed in the book of Revelation and elsewhere that terrible disaster would overwhelm them and they would be destroyed. It literally happened as anyone may read in the history of the Roman Empire. These events could be supplemented by many others down the centuries. The story of the Christian church in the Middle Ages, the story of the Protestant Reformation and the persecution of the Protestant Fathers illustrate the same principle. The devil, acting through the Roman church, tried to destroy the Protestants and for a time all seemed lost; but onward went the work of God. In the great stories of the Covenanters and of the Puritans are found further illustrations of the same great principle. By reviewing these things we, like Habakkuk, will be able to rejoice in the Lord in spite of circumstances.

Over and above all other facts is the most glorious fact of all, the fact of Jesus Christ himself. We are given the details of his earthly life in the Gospels so that we may have consolation in times of trouble. Above all remember that the Son of God himself has been through this world. He knows all about the contradiction of sinners against himself. Though he was the Son of God he knew what it was to be tired, to be weary, to be faint in his body, to sweat drops of blood in agony. He knew what it was to face the whole world and all the power of Satan and hell massed against himself. 'We have not an high priest which cannot be touched with the feeling of our infirmities; but was in all points tempted like as we are, yet without sin' (Hebrews 4:15). He knows all about our weakness and our frailty. The incarnation is not a mere idea but a fact: 'The Word was made flesh'. And in our agony and weakness we can always turn to him with confidence knowing that he understands, he knows, and he can succour. The Son of God became man in order that he might be our perfect High Priest and be able to lead us to God.

My hope is built on nothing less
Than Jesu's blood and righteousness.
I dare not trust my sweetest frame
But wholly lean on Jesu's Name.

When darkness seems to veil his face
I rest on his unchanging grace;
In every high and stormy gale
My anchor holds within the veil.

His oath, his covenant and blood
Support me in the 'whelming flood.
When all around my soul gives way
He then is all my hope and stay.
On Christ the solid Rock I stand.
All other ground is sinking sand.

So, come what may, 'I will rejoice in the Lord, I will joy in
the God of my salvation'.

Faith on Trial

CONTENTS

PREFACE

The 73rd Psalm deals with a problem that has often perplexed and discouraged God's people. It is a double problem – Why should the godly frequently have to suffer, especially in view of the fact that the ungodly frequently appear to be most prosperous?

It is a classic statement of the Bible's way of dealing with that problem. The Psalmist relates his own experience, exposes his soul to our gaze in a most dramatic manner, and leads us step by step from near-despair to final triumph and assurance. It is at the same time a grand theodicy. For these reasons it has always appealed to preachers and spiritual guides and counsellors.

The preparation and the preaching of the following sermons, expounding this rich teaching on successive Sunday mornings, was to me a labour of love and a true joy. The sermon entitled 'Nevertheless' in the series was used of God to bring immediate relief and great joy to a man who was in a great agony of soul and near breaking point. He had travelled some 6,000 miles and had reached London only the previous day. He was convinced, and still is, that God in his infinite grace had brought him that distance to hear that sermon.

May it and the others prove to be 'a door of hope' to many another whose feet are 'almost gone' and whose steps have 'well nigh slipped'.

D. M. LLOYD-JONES

PSALM 73

Truly God is good to Israel,
even to such as are of a clean heart.
But as for me, my feet were almost gone;
my steps had well nigh slipped.
For I was envious at the foolish,
when I saw the prosperity of the wicked.

For there are no bands in their death:
but their strength is firm.
They are not in trouble as other men;
neither are they plagued like other men.
Therefore pride compasseth them about as a chain;
violence covereth them as a garment.
Their eyes stand out with fatness:
they have more than heart could wish.
They are corrupt, and speak wickedly concerning oppression:
they speak loftily.
They set their mouth against the heavens,
and their tongue walketh through the earth.

Therefore his people return hither:
and waters of a full cup are wrung out to them.
And they say, How doth God know?
and is there knowledge in the most High?
Behold, these are the ungodly, who prosper in the world;
they increase in riches.
Verily I have cleansed my heart in vain,
and washed my hands in innocency.
For all the day long have I been plagued,
and chastened every morning.

If I say, I will speak thus;
behold, I should offend against the generation of thy children.
When I thought to know this,
it was too painful for me;
Until I went into the sanctuary of God;
then understood I their end.

70

Surely thou didst set them in slippery places:
thou castedst them down into destruction.
How are they brought into desolation, as in a moment!
they are utterly consumed with terrors.
As a dream when one awaketh;
so, O Lord, when thou awakest, thou shalt despise their image.

Thus my heart was grieved,
and I was pricked in my reins.
So foolish was I, and ignorant:
I was as a beast before thee.
Nevertheless I am continually with thee:
thou hast holden me by my right hand.
Thou shalt guide me with thy counsel,
and afterward receive me to glory.
Whom have I in heaven but thee?
and there is none upon earth that I desire beside thee.
My flesh and my heart faileth:
but God is the strength of my heart, and my portion for ever.

For, lo, they that are far from thee shall perish:
thou hast destroyed all them that go a whoring from thee.
But it is good for me to draw near to God:
I have put my trust in the Lord God,
that I may declare all thy works.

Chapter One

THE PROBLEM STATED

Truly God is good to Israel,
even to such as are of a clean heart.
But as for me, my feet were almost gone;
my steps had well nigh slipped.

The great value of the book of Psalms is that in it we have godly people stating their experience, and giving us an account of things that have happened to them in their spiritual life and warfare. Throughout history the book of Psalms has, therefore, been a book of great value for God's people. Again and again it provides them with the kind of comfort and teaching they need, and which they can find nowhere else. And it may well be, if one may be allowed to speculate on such a thing, that the Holy Spirit led the early church to adopt the Old Testament writings partly for that reason. What we find from the beginning to the end of the Bible is the account of God's dealings with his people. He is the same God in the Old Testament as in the New; and these Old Testament saints were citizens of the kingdom of God even as we are. We are taken into a kingdom which already contains such people as Abraham, Isaac and Jacob. The mystery that was revealed to the apostles was that the Gentiles should be fellow-heirs and citizens in the kingdom with the Jews.

It is right, therefore, to regard the experiences of these people as being exactly parallel with our own. The fact that

73

they lived in the old dispensation makes no difference. There is something wrong with a Christianity which rejects the Old Testament, or even with a Christianity which imagines that we are essentially different from the Old Testament saints. If any of you are tempted to feel like that, I would invite you to read the book of Psalms, and then to ask yourself whether you can honestly say from your experience some of the things the Psalmists said. Can you say, 'When my father and my mother forsake me, then the Lord will take me up'? Can you say, 'As the hart panteth after the water brooks, so panteth my soul after thee, O God'? Read the Psalms and the statements made in them, and I think you will agree that these people were children of God with a great and rich spiritual experience. For this reason, it has been the practice in the Christian church from the beginning for men and women to come to the book of Psalms for light and knowledge and instruction.

Its special value lies in the fact that it helps us by putting its teaching chiefly in the form of the recital of experiences. We have exactly the same teaching in the New Testament, only there it is given in a more didactic fashion. Here it seems to come down to our own ordinary and practical level. Now we are all familiar with the value of this. There are times when the soul is weary, when we feel we are incapable of receiving that more direct instruction; we are so tried, and our minds are so tired, and our hearts may be so bruised, that we somehow cannot make the effort to concentrate upon principles and to look at things objectively. It is at such a time, and particularly at such a time, and in order that they may receive truth in this more personal form, that people who feel that life has dealt cruelly with them have gone – battered and beaten by the waves and billows of life – to the Psalms. They have read the experiences of some of these people, and have found that they, too, have been through something very similar. And somehow that fact, in and of itself, helps and strengthens them. They feel that they are not alone, and that what is happening to them is not unusual. They begin to realize the truth of Paul's comforting words to the Corinthians, 'There hath no temptation taken you but such as is common to man,' and that very realization alone enables them to take courage and to be renewed in their faith. The book of Psalms is of inestimable value in this respect, and we find people turning constantly to it.

There are many features about the Psalms which might detain us. The thing I want to mention especially is the very remarkable honesty with which these writers do not hesitate to tell the truth about themselves. We have a great classic example of that here in the seventy-third Psalm. This man admits very freely that as for him his feet were almost gone, his steps had well-nigh slipped. And he goes on to say that he was like a beast before God, so foolish and so ignorant. What honesty! That is the great value of the Psalms. I know of nothing in the spiritual life more discouraging than to meet the kind of person who seems to give the impression that he or she is always walking on the mountain top. That is certainly not true in the Bible. The Bible tells us that these people knew what it was to be cast down, and to be in sore and grievous trouble. Many a saint in his pilgrimage has thanked God for the honesty of the writers of the Psalms. They do not just put up an ideal teaching which was not true in their own lives. Perfectionist teachings are never true. They are not true to the experience of the people who teach them, for we know that they are fallible creatures like the rest of us. They put their teaching of perfection forward theoretically, but it is not true to their experience. Thank God the Psalmists do not do that. They tell us the plain truth about themselves; they tell us the plain truth about what has happened to them.

Now their motive in doing so is not to exhibit themselves. Confession of sin can be a form of exhibitionism. There are some people who are very willing to confess their sins, so long as they can talk about themselves. It is a very subtle danger. The Psalmist does not do that; he tells us the truth about himself because he wants to glorify God. His honesty is dictated by that, for it is as he shows the contrast between himself and God that he ministers to the glory of God.

That is what this man does here. Notice that he starts off with a great triumphant note, 'Truly God is good to Israel, even to such as are of a clean heart,' as if to say, 'Now I am going to tell you a story; I am going to tell you what has

75

happened to me; but the thing I want to leave with you is just this – the goodness of God.' This comes out particularly clearly if you take another, and probably better, translation, 'God is always good to Israel, even to such as are of a clean heart.' God never varies. There is no limitation at all, there are no qualifications. 'This is my proposition,' says this man, 'God is always good to Israel.' Most of the Psalms start with some such great burst of praise and of thanksgiving.

Again, as has often been pointed out, the Psalms generally start with a conclusion. That sounds paradoxical, but I am not trying to be paradoxical: it is true. This man had had an experience. He went right through it and reached this point. Now the great thing to him was that he had arrived there. So he starts with the end; and then he proceeds to tell us how he got there. This is a good way of teaching; and it is always the method of the Psalms. The value of the experience is that it is an illustration of this particular truth. It is of no interest in and of itself, and the Psalmist is not interested in it as an experience *qua* experience. But it is an illustration of this great truth about God, and therein lies its value.

The great thing is that we should all realize this big point that he is making, namely, that God is always good to his people, to such as are of a clean heart. That is the proposition; but the thing that will engage us, as we study this Psalm in particular, is the method, the way, by which this man arrives at that conclusion. What he has to tell us can be summed up like this: He started from this proposition in his religious experience; then he went astray; then he came back again. It is because they analyse such experiences that we find the Psalms to be of such great value. We all know something about that same kind of experience in our own lives. We start in the right place; then something goes wrong, and we seem somehow to be losing everything. The problem is how to get back again. What this man does is to show us how to arrive back at that place where the soul finds her true poise.

This Psalm is only one illustration. You can find many others that do exactly the same thing. Take Psalm 43, for instance, where you find the Psalmist in a similar condition. He addresses himself, and says 'Why art thou cast down, O my soul? and why art thou disquieted within me?' He talks to himself, he addresses his soul. Now that is just what he is doing in Psalm 73, only here it is elaborated and brought before us in a very striking manner.

This man tells us all about a particular experience that he had passed through. He tells us that he was very badly shaken, and that he very nearly fell. What was the cause of his trouble? Simply that he did not quite understand God's way with respect to him. He had become aware of a painful fact. Here he was living a godly life; he was cleansing his heart, he tells us, and washing his hands in innocency. In other words, he was practising the godly life. He was avoiding sin; he was meditating upon the things of God; he was spending his time in prayer to God; he was in the habit of examining his life, and whenever he found sin he confessed it to God with sorrow, and he sought forgiveness and renewal. The man was devoting himself to a life which would be well-pleasing in God's sight. He kept clear of the world and its polluting effects; he separated himself from evil ways, and gave himself up to the living of this godly life. Yet, although he was doing all this, he was having a great deal of trouble, 'all the day long have I been plagued, and chastened every morning.' He was having a very hard and difficult time. He does not tell us exactly what was happening; it may have been illness, sickness, trouble in his family. Whatever it was, it was very grievous and hurtful; he was being tried, and tried very sorely. In fact, everything seemed to be going wrong and nothing seemed to be going right.

Now that was bad enough in itself. But that was not the thing that really troubled and distressed him. The real trouble was that when he looked at the ungodly he saw a striking contrast. 'These people,' he said, 'we all know to be ungodly – it is quite clear to everybody that they are ungodly. But they prosper in the world, they increase in riches, there are no bands – no pangs – in their death, but their strength is firm, they are not in trouble as others.' He gives this description of them in their arrogance, their deceitfulness, their blasphemy. He gives us the most perfect picture in all literature of the so-called successful man of the world. He even describes his posture, his arrogant appearance, with his eyes standing out with fatness, and his pride compassing him about as a chain

– a necklace. 'Violence covers them as a garment,' he says, 'they have more than heart could wish', 'they speak loftily' – what a perfect description it is.

Moreover, not only was it true of people who lived at the time of the Psalmist, but you see the same kind of person today. They make blasphemous statements about God. They say, 'How doth God know, and is there knowledge in the most High?' You talk about your God, they say; we don't believe in your God, yet look at us. Nothing goes wrong with us. But you, who are so godly, look at the things that happen to you! Now this was what caused this man his pain and his trouble. He believed God to be holy and righteous and true, one who intervenes on behalf of his people and surrounds them with loving care and wonderful promises. His problem was how to reconcile all this with what was happening to himself, and still more with what was happening to the ungodly.

This Psalm is a classic statement of this particular problem – God's ways with respect to mankind, and especially God's ways with respect to his own people. That was the thing that perplexed this psalmist as he contrasted his own lot with that of the wicked. And he tells us his reaction to it all.

Now let us content ourselves for the moment with drawing some general, but very important lessons from all this. The first comment which we must make is that perplexity in the light of this kind of situation is not surprising. This, I would say, is a fundamental principle, for we are dealing with the ways of Almighty God, and he has told us so often in his book, 'My thoughts are not your thoughts, neither are your ways my ways.' Half our trouble arises from the fact that we do not realize that that is the basic position from which we must always start. I think that many of us get into trouble just because we forget that we are really dealing with the mind of God, and that God's mind is not like our mind. We desire everything to be cut and dried and simple, and feel that there should never be any problems or difficulties. But if there is one thing that is taught more clearly than anything else in the Bible it is that that is never the case in our dealings with God. The ways of God are inscrutable; his mind is infinite and eternal, and his purposes are so great that our sinful minds cannot understand. Therefore, when such a Being is dealing with us, it ought not to surprise us if, at times, things take place which are perplexing to us.

We tend to think, of course, that God should be blessing his own children always, and that they should never be chastised. How often have we thought that! Did we not think it during the war? Why is it that God allows certain forms of tyranny to persist, especially those that are absolutely godless? Why does he not wipe them all out, and shower his blessings upon his own people? That is our way of thinking. But it is based on a fallacy. God's mind is eternal, and God's ways are so infinitely above us that we must always start by being prepared not to understand immediately anything he does. If we start with the other supposition, that everything should always be plain and clear, we shall soon find ourselves in the place where this man found himself. It is not surprising that when we look into the mind of the Eternal there should be times when we are given the impression that things are working out in a manner exactly opposite to what we think they ought to be.

Let me now put a second proposition. Perplexity in this matter is not only not surprising; I want to emphasize that to be perplexed is not sinful either. There, again, is something that is very comforting. There are those who give the impression that they think the ways of God are always perfectly plain and clear; they always seem to be able to reason thus, and the sky to them is always bright and shining, and they themselves are always perfectly happy. Well, all I can say is that they are absolutely superior to the apostle Paul, for he tells us in 2 Corinthians 4 that he was 'perplexed, but not in despair'. Ah yes, it is wrong to be in a state of despair; but it is not wrong to be perplexed. Let us draw this clear distinction; the mere fact that you may be perplexed about something that is happening at the present time does not mean that you are guilty of sin. You are in God's hand, and yet something unpleasant is happening to you, and you say: I do not understand. There is nothing wrong with that – 'perplexed, but not in despair'. The perplexity in and of itself is not sinful, for our minds are not only finite, they are also weakened by sin. We do not see things clearly; we do not know what is best for us; we cannot take the long view; so it is very natural that we should be perplexed.

Now although that is not sinful as far as it goes, we must hurry on to say that to be perplexed always opens the door to temptation. That is the real message of this Psalm. It is all right up to a point, but as soon as you get into this state of being perplexed, and you stop and dwell on it for a moment, at that moment temptation is at the door. It is ready to enter in, and before you know what has happened it will have entered in. And that is what had happened to this man.

That brings us to what the Psalmist tells us about the character of temptation and how important it is to recognize this. Temptation can be so powerful that not only does it shake the greatest and strongest saint; it does, indeed, get him down. 'As for me,' says this man of God, 'as for me, my feet were almost gone; my steps had well nigh slipped.'

'But that was in the Old Testament,' you say, 'and the Holy Spirit had not come then as he has come now. We are in the Christian position whereas this saint of God was not.' All right, if you like you may have it in the words of the apostle Paul, 'Wherefore let him that thinketh he standeth take heed lest he fall'! Paul, in explaining the Christian position to the Corinthians (1 Corinthians 10), goes back for an illustration to the Old Testament; and lest some of those superior people in Corinth might say: We have received the Holy Spirit, we are not like that, he says, 'Let him that thinketh he standeth take heed lest he fall.' The person who has not yet discovered the power of temptation is the veriest tyro in spiritual matters. Temptation can come with varying degrees of power and force. The Bible teaches that it comes sometimes to the most spiritual as a veritable hurricane sweeping all before it, with such terrific might that even a godly person is almost overwhelmed. Such is the power of temptation! But let me use again the words of the apostle: 'Take unto you the whole armour of God.' For you need it all. If you are to stand in the evil day you must be completely clothed with the whole armour of God. The might of the enemy against us is second only to the power of God. He is more powerful than any man who has ever lived; and the saints of the Old Testament went down before him. He tempted and tried the Lord Jesus Christ to the ultimate limit. Our Lord defeated him, but he alone has succeeded of all ever born of woman. Go back and read this Psalm again and you will see that temptation came when this man was least expecting it. It came in as the result of what was happening to him, it came through the door that was opened by the trouble he was experiencing, and by the contrast between that and the successful, apparently happy life of the ungodly.

The next point to note about temptation concerns its blinding effect. There is nothing more strange about temptation than the way in which, under its influence and power, we are made to do things that in our normal condition would be quite unthinkable to us. The Psalmist puts it like this – and notice that his wording is almost sarcasm at his own expense. Look at the third verse, 'For I was envious at the foolish.' He was envious of the arrogant. 'You know,' he seems to say, 'I hardly like to put it on paper, I am so heartily ashamed of it. But I have to confess that there was a moment when I, who have been so blessed of God, was envious of those ungodly people.' Only the blinding effect of temptation can explain that. It comes with such force that we are knocked off our balance, and are no longer able to think clearly.

Now there is nothing of more vital importance in this spiritual warfare than for us to realize that we are confronted by a power like that, and that therefore we cannot afford to relax for one moment. The thing is so powerful that it makes us see only what it wants us to see, and we forget everything else. This is the blinding effect of temptation!

Again, we must not forget the subtlety of Satan. He comes as a would-be friend. He had obviously come to the Psalmist like that. He said, 'Don't you think you are cleansing your heart in vain, and washing your hands in innocency?' As the well-known hymn puts it so perfectly:

> *Always fast and vigil?*
> *Always watch and prayer?*

'That is what you seem to be doing,' says the devil. 'You seem to be spending your time in self-denial and prayers. There is something wrong with this outlook of yours. You believe the gospel; but look at what is happening to you!

81

Why are you having this hard time? Why is a God of love dealing with you in this manner? Is that the Christian life you are advocating? My friend,' he says, 'you are making a mistake; you are doing yourself grievous damage and harm; you are not fair to yourself.' Oh, the terrible subtlety of it all.

Again there is the apparent logic of the case temptation presents. When it comes thus with its blinding effect it really does seem to be quite innocent and reasonable. 'After all,' it makes the Psalmist say, 'I am living a godly life, and this is what happens to me. Those other people are blaspheming God, and with "lofty" utterances are saying things which should never be thought, let alone said. Yet they are very prosperous; their children are all doing well; they have more than the heart could wish. Meanwhile I am suffering the exact opposite. There is only one conclusion to draw.' Looking at it from the natural human point of view, the case seems to be unanswerable. That is always a characteristic of temptation. No-one would ever fall to temptation if it were not. Its plausibility, its power, its strength, its logical and apparently unanswerable case. You know that I am not speaking theoretically. We all know something of this; if we do not, we are not Christian. This is the kind of thing to which God's people are subjected. Because they are God's people the devil makes a special target of them and seizes every opportunity to get them down.

At this point I would stress that to be tempted in that way is not sin. We must be clear about this. That such thoughts are put to us, and insinuated into our minds, does not mean that we are guilty of sin. Here again is something which is of fundamental importance in the whole matter of spiritual warfare. We must learn to draw a distinction between being tempted and sinning. You cannot control the thoughts that are put into your mind by the devil. He puts them there. Paul talks of 'the fiery darts of the wicked one'. Now that is what had been happening to the Psalmist. The devil had been hurling them at him, but the mere fact that they had been coming into his mind does not mean that he was guilty of sin. The Lord Jesus Christ himself was tempted. The devil put thoughts into his mind. But he did not sin, because he rejected them. Thoughts will come to you and the devil may try to press you to think that because thoughts have entered your mind you have sinned. But they are not your thoughts, they are the devil's – he put them there. It was the quaint Cornishman, Billy Bray, who put this in his own original manner when he said, 'You cannot prevent the crow from flying over your head, but you can prevent him from making a nest in your hair!' So I say that we cannot prevent thoughts being insinuated into our mind; but the question is what do we do with them? We talk about thoughts 'passing through' the mind, and so long as they do this, they are not sin. But if we welcome them and agree with them then they become sin. I emphasize this because I have often had to deal with people who are in great distress because unworthy thoughts have come to them. But what I say to them is this, 'Listen to what you are telling me. You say that the thought "has come to you". Well, if that is true you are not guilty of sin. You do not say, "I have thought"; you say, "the thought came". That is right. The thought came to you, and it came from the devil, and the fact that the thought did come from the devil means that you are not of necessity guilty of sin.' Temptation, in and of itself, is not sin.

That brings us to the last and very vital point. It is that we should know how to deal with temptation when it comes, that we should know how to handle it. Indeed, in one sense the writer's whole purpose is just to tell us this. There is only one way in which we can be quite sure that we have dealt with temptation in the right way, and that is that we arrive at the right ultimate conclusion. I started with that and I end with it. The great message of this Psalm is, that if you and I know what to do with temptation we can turn it into a great source of victory. We can end, when we have been through a process like this, in a stronger position than we were in at the beginning. We may have been in a situation where our 'steps had well nigh slipped'. That does not matter so long as, at the end, we arrive on that great high plateau where we stand face to face with God with an assurance we have not had before. We can make use of the devil and all his assaults: but we have to learn how to handle him. We can turn all this into a great spiritual victory, so that we can say, 'Well, having been through it all, I have now been given to see that God is always good. I was tempted to think there were times when he was not; I see now that that was wrong. God is always good in all circumstances, in all ways, at all times – no matter what may happen to me, or to anybody else.' 'I have arrived,' says the Psalmist, 'at the conclusion that "God is always good to Israel".'

Are we all ready to say that? Some of you may be passing through this kind of experience at this moment. Things may be going wrong with you, and you may be having a hard time. Blow upon blow may be descending upon you. You have been living the Christian life, reading your Bible, working for God, and yet the blows have come, one on top of another. Everything seems to be going wrong; you have been plagued 'all the day long', and 'chastened every morning'. One trouble follows hard after another. Now the one simple question I want to ask is this. Are you able to say in the face of it all, 'God is always good'? Yes, even in the face of what is happening to you, and even as you see the wicked flourish. In spite of the cruelty of an enemy or the treachery of a friend, in spite of all that is happening to you, can you say, 'God is always good; there is no exception; there is no qualification'? Can you say that? Because if you cannot, then you are guilty of sin. You may have been tempted to doubt. That is to be expected; that is not sin. The question is, Were you able to deal with the temptation? Were you able to thrust it back, and to put it out of your mind? Were you able to say, 'God is always good,' without any reservation at all? Are you able to say, 'All things work together for good,' without any hesitation? That is the test. But let me remind you that while the Psalmist says, 'God is always good to Israel,' he is careful to add, 'Even to such as are of a clean heart.' Now we must be careful. We must be fair to ourselves; we must be fair to God. The promises of God are great, and all-inclusive. But they always have this condition, 'to them that are of a clean heart'. In other words, if you and I are sinning against God, then God will have to deal with us, and it is going to be painful. But even when God chastises us he is still good to us. It is because he is good to us that he chastises us. If we do not experience chastisement, then we are 'bastards', as the author of the Epistle of the Hebrews reminds us. But, let us remember, if we want to see this clearly we must be of a clean heart. We must have 'truth in [our] inward parts', and there must be no hidden sin, because 'If I regard iniquity in my heart, the Lord will not hear me.' If I am not true and straight with God I have no right to appropriate any of the promises. If, on the other hand, it is my one desire to be right with him, then I can say that it is absolutely the case that 'God is always good to Israel'.

I sometimes think that the very essence of the whole Christian position, and the secret of a successful spiritual life, is just to realize two things. They are in these first two verses, 'Truly God is good to Israel, even to such as are of a clean heart. But as for me, my feet were almost gone; my steps had well nigh slipped.' In other words, I must have complete, absolute confidence in God, and no confidence in myself. As long as you and I are in the position in which we 'worship God in the Spirit, and rejoice in Christ Jesus, and have no confidence in the flesh' all is well with us. That is to be truly Christian – on the one hand utter absolute confidence in God, and on the other no confidence in myself and what I may do. If I take that view of myself, it means that I shall always be looking to God. And in that position I shall never fail.

May God grant us grace to apply some of these simple principles to ourselves and, as we do so, let us remember that we have the greatest and the grandest illustration of it all in our blessed Lord himself. I see him in the Garden of Gethsemane, the very Son of God, and I hear him uttering these words, 'Father, if it be possible.' There was perplexity. He asked, Is there no other way, is this the only way whereby mankind can be saved? The thought of the sin of the world coming between him and his Father perplexed him. But he humbled himself. The perplexity did not cause him to fall, he just committed himself to God saying in effect, 'Thy ways are always right, thou art always good, and as for what thou art going to do to me I know it is because thou art good. Not my will, but thine, be done.'

Chapter Two

GETTING A FOOT-HOLD

If I say, I will speak thus;
behold, I should offend against the
generation of thy children.

We have seen that the conclusion arrived at by the Psalmist was that God is always good to Israel, to those who are of a clean heart, to those who really are concerned about pleasing him. We come back to this now in order that we may discover together the way in which the Psalmist managed to steady himself and to arrive back eventually at such a great and firm position of faith. There is nothing more profitable when reading a Psalm than to analyse it in the way we are proposing to do. The common tendency is just to read the Psalm through and be content with mere general effects. There are many people who use the Psalms like drugs. They will tell you that they always find that in trouble or perplexity it is a good thing to read one of them. 'There is something so peaceful about them,' they say, 'and the language is so soothing. As you read "The Lord is my Shepherd", it has a kind of general psychological effect upon you; it puts you into a wonderful state of mind and peace of heart, and you find that you have gone off to sleep without knowing it.' It is good psychological treatment. There are people who use the Psalms like that. There are others who use them as poetry. Their chief interest lies in the beauty of the language. Now the Psalms have all that, but I am concerned to show that primarily they are the recital of spiritual experiences which are meant for our profit. We shall never gain that profit from the Psalms, however, if

we do not take the trouble to analyse them, if we do not take
the trouble to observe what the Psalmist means. We have to
forget, for the moment, the beauty of the words, as such,
and concentrate on the meaning. As we do so we shall
discover that he has a very definite method.

This man, in this particular Psalm, did not suddenly arrive
at his position; he reached it as the result of a number of
things that had gone before. There were steps in the process
which are of real interest, and the profitable thing for us is
to discover these steps, which brought the man from the
position where his 'feet were almost gone' back to that firm
condition of faith in which he was unshakable and immovable.
It is most important for us to realize that there is such a thing
as 'the discipline of the Christian life'. It is not enough to
say, as so many do, that, whatever may happen to us, we
have just to 'look to the Lord' and all will be well. I assert
that that is not true, and that it is not true in the experience
of the people who teach it. It is unscriptural teaching. Were
that the only thing we have to do, many of these scriptures
would be quite unnecessary; we would not need them at all.
If all we have to do is 'just to look to the Lord' the Epistles
need never have been written; but they have been written,
and they were written by men inspired by the Holy Spirit.
Why? The answer is that they were written for our instruction, in order to teach us how to live, and what they tell us,
in a sense, is that there is an essential *discipline* in the Christian
life.

One of the saddest features in the lives of certain types of
Christian at the present time is that they seem to have lost
sight of this aspect of the faith. This is, alas, especially true
of those who are evangelical, and I think I understand why
this is so. First and foremost there was a reaction against
Roman Catholic teaching. In the Roman Catholic system they
make a great deal of a certain type of discipline. They have
many handbooks and manuals on the subject. In fact, some
of the greatest masters in this kind of teaching have been
Roman Catholics as, for instance, Saint Bernard of Clairvaux,
or the well-known Fénélon, whose famous *Letters to Men*
and *Letters to Women* were very popular at one time.

Now Protestants have reacted against all that, and to some

extent very rightly. For there is no question at all but that in the Roman Catholic system the method becomes more important than the spiritual life itself, and its observer becomes a slave to method. As Protestants it is right that we should protest against that entirely. But to deduce from its misuse that there is no need for discipline at all in the Christian life is quite wrong.

In fact, the really great periods in Protestantism have always been characterized by the realization of the need for such discipline. If there was one thing more than anything else that characterized the great Puritan period it was the attitude and the outlook that led Richard Baxter to write his *Spiritual Directory*. The Puritans were concerned to teach people how to apply the Scriptures to daily life. And in the next century we find that the leaders of the Evangelical Awakening emphasized the same thing. Why were men like the two Wesley brothers and Whitefield called Methodists? They were so called because they were methodical in their living. They were Methodists because they had method in their meetings. They drew up certain rules; they formed their Societies, and they insisted that all who desired to belong to the Society should do certain things and not do other things. The very term Methodist is most expressive. It emphasizes the fact that they believed in discipline and in the importance of disciplining one's life and of knowing how to deal with oneself and how to handle oneself in the various circumstances and situations that we meet in the world we live in.

Here in this Psalm we have a great master in this respect. The man who wrote it has a very definite method, and we cannot do better than look at it. He teaches us how to handle ourselves – how to manage ourselves. Is that not one of the major problems of life for each one of us in this world? Is it not the most difficult task for any one of us to manage ourself? It is much easier for us to manage everybody else! The great art in the Christian life is to know how to handle oneself, especially in certain critical situations. Here, this man lets us into the secret.

Let us start, then, with the first step, the lowest of all. I feel that there is something very wonderful in what he tells us. Here is a great man, one who had experienced unusual blessings, and yet the first thing that held him and saved him from disaster is indeed most surprising. Our reaction to the discovery of what this first step was in his process of recovery will be a very good test of our spiritual understanding. I wonder if there will be any who will feel that this is too low a plane, that no Christian ought to stand on such a level? Let us examine ourselves as we follow what this man has to say.

As we start at this very lowest level, let me say that I do not care very much where we take our stand, so long as we take it; I do not care how low our stand is, so long as we are standing and not sliding. It is better to stand on the lowest rung of the ladder than to be down in the depths. Now this man started at the very bottom, and from there he began to ascend. How did he do it? Let us first of all consider the method – exactly what he did – and then from that let us deduce certain principles which we can lay down as being always applicable to any situation in which we may find ourselves.

Here is a man suddenly tempted, tempted to say something, or, if you like, tempted to do something. The force of the temptation is so great that he is almost thrown off his balance. He is on the point of falling to the temptation, and he tells us what it was that saved him. Here it is, 'If I say' – he was on the point of saying something – 'If I say, I will speak thus; behold, I should offend against the generation of thy children.' What does he do? What is his method?

The first thing he does is to take himself in hand. I do not think he knew quite why he was doing it, but he did it. He just kept himself from saying what was on the tip of his tongue. It was there, but he did not say it. Now this is tremendously important. The Psalmist realized the importance of never speaking hurriedly, of never speaking on an impulse. That was the first thing, and it is a very general point. It is a perfectly good point for a person to make who is not a Christian at all, and that is the very thing I am suggesting – namely, that there are things which we have to do in connection with this spiritual discipline that at first sight do not seem to be particularly Christian. But if they hold you, use them.

There are many people who are so anxious to be always

on the mountain top in a spiritual sense that for that very reason they often find themselves falling down into the valley. They disregard these ordinary methods. They do not avoid doing what the man who wrote Psalm 116 had done. You remember what he tells us. He makes a very honest confession. He says, 'I said in my haste, All men are liars.' He said that in his haste, and that was the mistake. This man in Psalm 73 had discovered, even when he was on the point of falling, the importance of not saying anything in haste. It is wrong for a Christian to say or do anything in haste. If you want it in its New Testament garb here it is from the Epistle of James, 'Be swift to hear, slow to speak, slow to wrath' (James 1:19). I must not elaborate on this here, but is it not obvious that if only we all implemented this particular principle then life would be much more harmonious? What a lot of trouble would be saved! What a lot of pin-pricks and irritations, what a lot of quarrelling and backbiting and unhappiness would be avoided in every realm of life, if only we all heeded this injunction! 'Be swift to hear, slow to speak'! Stop and think. If you can do nothing else, stop! Do not act on impulse. This man did not. It was the first thing that prevented him from falling.

The next step obviously was that he considered and faced again what he was about to say. The problem was there in his mind; it seemed as if no-one could gainsay it, the facts were so obvious. There are the ungodly; I see their prosperity; and here am I always in trouble. It seems so obvious – shall I say it? 'No,' says the Psalmist, 'have another look at it, examine it again. When it is something like this, you cannot examine it too frequently.' He began to talk to himself about it. He put it before him. He looked at it again. Oh, what a vital thing that is. How many tragedies would have been avoided in life if people would only take one further look. In the matter of temptation, when it comes with its blinding force, and when every argument seems to be on the one side and not one on the other, the whole strategy of fighting the devil is to insist upon having this one further view. And that one view will probably save you. He looked at it again, he turned it round, he examined it from different angles.

The Psalmist's action shows that he was considering the

consequences of what he was about to say. Here again is a great principle. Nothing that we do in this life is without its consequences. Every effect has a cause, and every cause produces an effect. So many of our troubles arise from the fact that we forget that causes lead to effects, and that these effects in turn lead to certain inevitable consequences. The devil traps us in his subtlety by seizing on what appears to be the isolated event. He puts that one thing before us in such a manner that we can see and think of nothing else. This one thing monopolizes our attention and the consequences are not considered. But this man saw the consequences. He said, 'If I say, I will speak thus; behold, I should offend against the generation of thy children.' He was careful to consider the consequences, and to confront himself with them.

The Bible gives us many instances of this. One of the most glorious examples of it, I think, is in the case of that man Nehemiah. Nehemiah was in a position where his life was in jeopardy and a false 'friend' came to him and said, 'You are a very good man, and therefore you must not risk your life in the way you are doing – "in the night will they come to slay thee".' He suggested a proposal whereby Nehemiah should flee, and he put it in terms which sounded ingratiating and full of concern. If Nehemiah had listened to him the whole course of Israel's history would have been changed. The proposition must have appealed to him, but Nehemiah pulled himself up by saying, 'Should such a man as I flee?' He considered the consequences, and the moment he saw the consequences he did not do what was suggested. That is the thing that saved this man in Psalm 73. He saw the consequences and immediately he refrained.

Let us go a step farther. The next thing was that this man held on to what he was certain of, and he held on at all costs. About his main problem he was very uncertain; he could not understand that at all. Even after he had pulled himself up, it still puzzled him; he could not understand or grasp it. But having looked at the thing again he realized that if he were to speak as he was tempted to speak, the immediate consequence would be that he would be the cause of offence to God's people, and he held on to that fact. Here then is the principle.

The Psalmist is not sure about this whole question of God's dealing with his children. That is still a matter of great perplexity. But he is very sure that it is wrong to be a stumbling-block or cause of offence to the generation of God's children. He is absolutely certain of that, and he acts upon it. You see the strategy. When you are uncertain and perplexed, the thing to do is to try to find something of which you are certain, and then take your stand on that. It may not be the central thing; that does not matter. This man saw the consequences of what he was about to do, and he knew for certain it was wrong. Therefore he said, 'I will not say it.' He is still not clear about the main trouble, but he is clear about that.

The last interim decision this man arrived at was that he would have to be content not to solve his main problem for the time being. He tells us that he was still not clear about, and still could not understand, the difficulty that had shaken him and tempted him so severely. And indeed, he did not understand it until he went into the sanctuary of God. So he stopped trying to solve it, saying to himself, 'Well, I must leave this main problem for the time being. I will say nothing about it because I can see that if I express my thoughts it will cause me to offend against the generation of God's people. And I cannot do that. Very well; I will take my stand on what I am certain of, and be content not to understand the other matter for the present.' That is his method. That was the thing that saved him; that was what helped him.

How simple his method is, and yet how vital is every single step. Let me put it in the form of a number of principles. The first principle I would lay down for our special guidance is that our speech must always be essentially positive. I mean that we should never be too ready to express our doubts and to proclaim our uncertainties. I have met people who have spent many years of their lives in agony of soul because of things they had said years before when they were not Christian, things which had been the means of shaking the faith of others. That is a terrible thing. I remember a young man coming to me years ago. He was a student who had gone to his college grounded in the Christian faith and believing it. A Professor in that college who prided himself on being an unbeliever, and who had nothing positive to give that young man, would ridicule him and his position, not only in his lectures but in private, laughing at all his beliefs and pouring scorn upon his faith. It had landed this young man in a very grievous and unhappy condition. There are not many things worse than the action of such a Professor who, having nothing himself by which to live, tries to take away and to destroy the faith of a young man, speaking against it and trying to undermine it. This, of course, was a malicious and intentional attack on a young man's faith. But we, too, can be guilty of the same thing, although we may not be aware of it. Though we may be assailed by doubts or uncertainties, we ought not to proclaim our doubts, or voice our uncertainties (except, of course, to seek help for ourselves), lest our words, too, unwittingly have the same disastrous effect. If we can say nothing helpful we should say nothing at all. That was what this man did. He could not understand, and he was on the point of saying something, but he said, 'I will not. If I say a thing like that I shall damage these people of God.' Say what you like about this man, he was at any rate a gentleman. If you find your Christian faith shaking, at any rate be a gentleman. Do not harm anyone else. We must learn to discipline ourselves and not to pass on our difficulties and talk so much about our uncertainties. This man said nothing until he was able to say, 'God is always good to Israel.' He is entitled to speak then. Having started with that, he can then safely go on to tell the story of his troubles.

The next principle is that truth is comprehensive and its various parts interrelated. I mean that there is no such thing as isolated truth. This man started off by thinking there was only one problem, the problem of the prosperity of the ungodly. But interrelated with that was this other truth about God's people and what happens to them. Let me give you another illustration to show the importance of realizing this principle that all aspects of the truth are interrelated. Very often people who are scientifically inclined get into difficulties over their faith because they forget this principle. They are confronted by what purports to be scientific evidence. Something is offered to them by scientists as a fact, and the danger is that they will accept that particular statement as it stands, without realizing the consequences of that acceptance in another department of truth. For instance, I always say that one very good reason for rejecting the theory of evolution is that the moment I accept it I am in trouble and difficulty with the doctrine of sin, and the doctrine of faith, and the doctrine of the atonement. Truth is interrelated; one thing affects another. Do not be too ready to form opinions on one fact or one set of facts. Remember that it will affect other facts and other positions. Look at the subject from every conceivable aspect, bearing in mind not only the thing itself but also its consequences and implications. Take them all in before you express an opinion.

The next principle is that we must never forget our relationship to one another. The thing that held this man at first was not anything that he discovered about God's way with respect to himself but his recollection of his relationship to other people. That is marvellous, I think. That is the thing that held this man. It was something he was sure about, and he held on to it. The apostle Paul puts that in a striking verse in Romans 14. He says, 'None of us liveth to himself, and no man dieth to himself.' He goes on to elaborate it, and in doing so analyses the question of the weaker brother. He does the same in 1 Corinthians 8 and 10. He puts it like this in a most remarkable phrase, 'Conscience, I say, not thine own, but of the other' (10:29). In other words, you as a strong Christian must not decide this in terms of yourself. What about your weaker brother for whom Christ died? You must not offend his conscience. No man 'liveth unto himself'; we are all bound up together, and if you cannot check yourself for your own sake, you must check yourself because of your weaker brother. When you are next tempted, when the devil makes you forget that you are not an isolated case, when he suggests that this is something that concerns you alone, think of the consequences, remember the other people, remember Christ, remember God. If you and I fall, it is not an isolated fall, the whole church falls with us. This man realized that he was bound in the bundle of life with these other people. Say then to yourself, 'I see that all these others are going to be involved. We are children of a heavenly kingdom, we are individual members, in particular, of the one Body of Christ.

95

We cannot act in isolation.' So if nothing else checks you when you are about to do something wrong, remember that fact, remember your family, remember the people to whom you belong, remember the Name that is on your forehead, and if nothing else will hold you, let that hold you. It held this man.

The next principle is the importance of having certain absolutes in our life. In other words, we must learn to recognize that there are certain things that are quite unthinkable, and we must never do them. We should make it our business in life to list certain things that must never be done. We must never even consider them. I do not hesitate to assert that the appalling increase in divorce cases at the present time is simply due to the failure to realize this principle. I mean that when two people marry and take their solemn vows and pledges before God and before others they ought to be locking a certain back door that they should never even look at again. But that is not the way today. People seem to get married and to leave the back door, which leads to separate lives, open. They are looking backwards over their shoulder, and they often allow themselves to think of the possibility of breaking up the marriage before they have even made their vows. That is why life is as it is at the present time. People no longer have their absolutes.

At one time such a thing was unthinkable; it should always be unthinkable. There are certain things Christian men and women must put down as unthinkable absolutes, never to be considered. This man had one principle if he had nothing else at this point, and on this one point he stood. He said, 'I will never say anything that is going to make my brethren unhappy. I do not care how much I fail to understand; one of my absolutes is this, I am never going to harm my brethren.' He stood on that resolutely and eventually he began to understand his own perplexities. Let us get our absolutes fixed, let us get certain things established irrevocably. I say to young people especially – although it does not apply to you more than to anybody else, yet while you are young and are not guilty in these things – put down your absolutes. If you cannot be helpful, say nothing. Never do God's cause or your spiritual family any harm.

The last principle is the importance of remembering who and what you are. In a sense I have already covered this. You and I are people who have been called by God out of this present evil world. We have been purchased at the cost of the shed blood of the only begotten Son of God on a cross on Calvary's hill, not merely that we may be forgiven and go to heaven, but that we may be delivered from all sin and iniquity, and that he may 'purify unto himself a peculiar people, zealous of good works' (Titus 2:14). He has done that, and that is our claim. I say, therefore, remember that, and whenever any perplexity arises or anything that tends to shake you, take it and put it in the light of that. Though you do not understand the thing itself, you must at that point say, 'I do not mind, I am content not to understand. All I know is that as a child of God, bought with the blood of Christ, there are certain things that I cannot do and this is one of them, and therefore I will not do it, and whatever the consequences are, I will stand firm.'

Those, then, are my conclusions. It does not matter at what level we stand against this enemy of our souls, it does not matter how low the level, so long as we stand. As I said at the outset, this man stood at a very low level. He simply stood on the one principle, 'If I do thus, I shall harm these people.' He could not have stood on a much lower level than that. I do not care how low the level is. So long as you can find anything that will hold you, use it. Do not despise 'the day of small things'. Do not think that you are too spiritual to stand on such a low level. If you do, you will fall. Stand on any point you can. Stand even on a negative – I mean by that, that you may be capable of saying only, 'I could not do that.' Stand on that. For it comes to this, when your feet are slipping the one thing you need is to be able to stand. Stop slipping and sliding. Get your feet firm for a moment and take anything that offers itself for that purpose; stand on that and stay on that. We are engaged in spiritual mountaineering. The slopes are like glass, and you can slip into that terrible ravine and lose yourself. I say, therefore, that if you see anything, however small a twig, clutch at it, hold it, put your feet in the slightest hole, or on the narrowest ledge, anything to steady yourself and to enable you to stop for the moment.

Once you have stopped the downward slipping and sliding you can begin to climb again.

It was because the Psalmist found that small foothold and planted his feet in it, that he stopped slipping. And from that moment he began the wonderful process of climbing again until eventually he found himself able to rejoice once more in the knowledge of God and to understand even the problem that had perplexed him, and to say, 'God is always good to Israel. What a fool I have been.'

Chapter Three

THE IMPORTANCE OF SPIRITUAL THINKING

When I thought to know this,
it was too painful for me;
Until I went into the sanctuary of God;
then understood I their end.

So far, we have arrived at the conclusion that in a spiritual conflict it does not matter at all at what low level you arrest your fall, so long as you do arrest it. Do not disdain the lower level. It is better to have your feet on the lowest rung of the ladder than to be on the ground: it is better to find the smallest foothold than to be sliding down a slippery slope: for it is by climbing from there that you will eventually find yourself at the top.

But now we must proceed, because obviously the Psalmist did not stop there. If he had stopped there, he would never have written his Psalm at all, and he could not have said, 'God is always good to Israel.' The foothold was only the beginning. There are still various further steps in this marvellous process, because, even after having got his foothold, he was still very unhappy. He understood enough to say, 'If I say I will speak thus; behold, I should offend against the generation of thy children.' But still he says, 'When I thought to know this, it was too painful for me.' Though he is no longer slipping he still does not understand his main problem. But he is no longer going down, he is no longer in danger of uttering those terrible blasphemous thoughts.

He was still, however, in great anguish of mind and heart;

he still had his perplexity about God's ways with him. I do want to emphasize that, because it is a very vital matter. Though the great thing and the first thing is to stop slipping, that does not mean that you are now all right or that from that moment you are quite clear about your problem. This man was not clear, he was in real trouble still. Thank God, he knows enough to prevent his going down, but his problem is as acute as it was before. Do you know that spiritual position? Have you ever been there? I have been there many a time. It is a strange place to be in, but in many ways a wonderful one. You have something vital holding you, though your original problem is as definite as it was at the beginning.

What he tells us is this. He was standing there; he was no longer slipping; the rebellious thoughts were under control. But his thoughts were going round and round in circles, and he was in great anguish of mind and of heart. This continued, he tells us, until he 'went into the sanctuary of God'. 'Then understood I their end.' Now there is one point which I must make clear before we go any farther. If you look up the various translations of this Psalm you will find that some of them suggest that this should be translated, 'It was too painful for me until I entered into the secret of God,' instead of 'until I went into the sanctuary of God'. But the reasons for keeping 'sanctuary' here seem to me to be quite overwhelming. One good reason is that all the Psalms in this section of the Psalter deal with the literal place, the sanctuary. Read the next Psalm and Psalm 76 and you will find that each of them has reference to the literal, physical, material sanctuary. It seems to me that this in itself is conclusive, quite apart from other evidence which can be produced. However, it is a point which is quite immaterial, because when someone went into the Tabernacle or the Temple of God he did enter into the presence of God. The people under the old dispensation when they went to the Temple went there to meet with God. It was the place in which God's honour dwelt; it was the place where the Shekinah glory of God was present. This man was certainly entering into the presence of God, but I think it is important to remember that sanctuary here literally means the building. 'Until I went into the sanctuary of God; then understood I.'

He was unhappy; he was perplexed; it was an awful problem. But once he went into the sanctuary of God everything became clear to him. He was put right, and he began to climb up the ladder again, until eventually he reached the top and could say, 'God is always good to Israel' – without exception.

There are certain very vital lessons for us in this particular section. Here is a man who has gained a foothold and now is beginning to ascend. What are the lessons? The first I would suggest is the absolute necessity in the Christian life of being able to think spiritually. Let me explain what I mean. The whole trouble with the Psalmist up till now was that he had been approaching his problem solely in terms of his own thoughts and his own understanding. That, he tells us, was a complete failure. He had before him two factors – the prosperity of the ungodly, and the troubles and problems and miseries of the godly, especially himself. His thoughts ran something like this, 'This situation is quite plain and uncomplicated. It is not in the least involved. Facts, after all, are facts, and you cannot ignore them. And what a practical, common-sense man of the world does is to look at facts. That being so, there is obviously something wrong. I know all about the promises of God; but what has happened to them in this situation? How can I possibly be like this, and the ungodly like that, if the message of God's word is right and true?

Now he had been reasoning in that way, and he had come back to the same position time and time again. You all know the process, do you not? You start thinking about the problem and you go round and round in circles. You try to forget it by plunging into business, or pleasure, or something else. Then you go to bed at night, and you start all over again, 'Things are going badly with me and well with the ungodly.' And you go round and round the same circle again. You say, 'Could it be that I am making a mistake here? No, I am not; the facts are obvious.' That was the Psalmist's position. What was the matter? I say that the whole essence of this man's trouble was that he was thinking rationally only, instead of spiritually.

This is a tremendously important principle. It is very difficult to put into language the difference between purely

rational thinking and spiritual thinking, because someone may
be tempted to say, 'Ah, yes, there it is again. I have always
said that Christian thinking is irrational.' But that is a false
deduction. While I draw a distinction between rational
thinking and spiritual thinking, I am not for a moment
suggesting that spiritual thinking is irrational. The difference
between them is that rational thinking is on ground-level
only; spiritual thinking is equally rational, but it takes in a
higher level as well as the lower level. It takes in all the facts
instead of merely some of them. I shall develop that later,
but I state it like that now in order that it may make clear
what I mean by contrasting merely rational thinking with
spiritual thinking.

With this in mind I want to enunciate certain principles.
First, there is a constant danger of our slipping back to merely
rational thinking even in our Christian life. This is a very
subtle thing. Without realizing it at all, though we are Christian, though we are born again, though we have the Holy
Spirit in us, there is the constant danger of our reverting to
a type of thinking that has nothing to do with Christianity
at all. The Psalmist was a devout and godly man, one who
had had great experience at the hand of God; but quite unconsciously he had reverted to that merely rational type of
thinking. Perhaps I can put this point still more clearly by
saying that we have to learn that the whole of the Christian
life is spiritual and not merely parts of it.

Every Christian, of course, will agree with this, and will
recognize at once that from the beginning the Christian view
of life is something which is altogether different from the
rational way of looking at life. Take what Paul tells us in 1
Corinthians 2. He asks, in effect, why it is that some people
are not Christian, why it was that the princes of this world
did not recognize the Lord Jesus Christ when he was here.
The answer, he says, is that they had not received the Holy
Spirit. They looked at him only on the rational level. They
saw nothing but a peasant; they saw nothing but a carpenter;
they saw one who had not been trained in the school of the
Pharisees, and they said that this man could not be the Son
of God. Why? Because they were indulging in purely rational
thinking. They were doing what I have suggested to you this

Psalmist was doing at this point.

The case of the princes of this world and the case of all who do not believe in Christ is still this. For them Jesus of Nazareth was only a man who was born and laid in a manger, lived, ate and drank like other people and worked as a carpenter. Then he was crucified in utter weakness upon a cross. 'There are the facts,' they say, 'and am I asked to believe that that is the Son of God? It is impossible.' What is wrong with them? They are thinking only on the rational level. They believe in the theory of evolution, and faced with the account of supernatural events, they say, 'Things like that do not happen in the evolutionary process; things like that are impossible.' That is rational thinking. You talk to them about the doctrine of the rebirth, and they say, 'Of course things like that don't happen, there is no such thing as a miracle. We see laws in nature; but once you talk about miracles you are violating the laws of nature.' As Matthew Arnold said, 'Miracles cannot happen, therefore miracles have not happened.' That is rational thinking.

Now we all agree that before someone can become a Christian he has to cease to think like that. He has to have a new type of thinking, he has to begin to think spiritually. The first thing that happens to us when we become Christian is that we find that we are thinking in a different way. We are on a different level. In other words, as soon as we start thinking spiritually, miracles are no longer a problem, the rebirth is no longer a problem, the doctrine of the atonement is no longer a problem. We have a new understanding, we are thinking spiritually. Our Lord was visited by Nicodemus, who came by night and said, 'Master, I have watched your miracles; you must be a Teacher sent from God, for no man can do the things you do except God be with him.' And he was clearly on the point of adding, 'Tell me how you do it; what is the explanation?' But our Lord looked at him and said, 'Verily, verily, I say unto thee, Except a man be born again, he cannot see the kingdom of God,' and 'Ye must be born again.' What he was saying to Nicodemus was really this, 'Nicodemus, if you think that you can understand this thing before it has happened to you, you are making a real mistake. You will never become a Christian in that way. You

103

are thinking rationally, you are trying to understand spiritual things with your natural understanding. But you cannot. Though you are a master of Israel you must be born again. You have to become as a little child if you want to enter this kingdom. You have to cease to rely on this power of thought which you have as a natural man, and you have to realize the nature of this new type of thinking which is spiritual. You must be born again.'

All who are Christian will agree with that and understand it. We say that the trouble with people who are not Christian is just that they will not surrender that natural way of thinking in which they have always been brought up, and in which they have been trained and to which they have given themselves. Yes; but the point I am making is that you have to make that surrender not only at the beginning of your Christian life, not merely in the matter of forgiveness of sins and the rebirth. The whole of the Christian life is spiritual, not merely parts of it, not only the beginning.

Now the trouble with so many of us, as it was with this Psalmist of old, is that although we have come into the Christian life, and have started on a spiritual level, we have then dropped back to the rational with regard to particular problems. Instead of thinking of them spiritually we go back and think of them as though we were merely natural men and women. It is something that tends to happen to us during the whole of our Christian lives. I have often listened to Christian people who are in some perplexity and, even as they have been stating their problem, I have realized that their trouble was wholly due to the fact that they had dropped back to the rational level of thinking. For instance, when something happens to you that you do not understand, the moment you begin to feel a sense of grudge against God you may be sure that you have already dropped back to that rational level. When you complain that what is happening to you does not seem to be fair, you are at once bringing God down to your own level of understanding. That is exactly what this man did. But everything in the Christian life must be regarded from the spiritual angle. The whole of this life is spiritual. Everything about us must therefore be considered spiritually, every phase, every stage, every interest, every development.

Or let me put it like this. Ultimately the problems and difficulties of the Christian life are all spiritual, so that the moment we enter this realm we must think in a spiritual way and leave the other mode of thinking behind. That is especially true with regard to the whole problem of understanding God's ways with respect to us. That was this man's problem. Why does God allow these things? he says. Why are the ungodly allowed to prosper? If God is God, why does he not wipe them off the face of the earth? And, on the other hand, if God is God, why does he allow me to suffer as I am suffering at the present time? That was the problem, trying to understand God's ways. Now in the last analysis there is only one answer to that. It is found in Isaiah 55:8, 'For my thoughts are not your thoughts, neither are your ways my ways, saith the Lord.' That is the ultimate answer. The first thing you have to realize, God says to us, is that when you come to consider me and my ways, you must not do so on that low level to which you have been accustomed, because my thoughts are higher than your thoughts and my ways are higher than your ways. But, even as Christian people, are we not constantly guilty here? We will persist in thinking as natural men and women in these matters. We see that the matter of salvation calls for spiritual thinking, but in the things that happen to us our thinking is prone to become rational thinking again, and we must not be surprised therefore if we do not understand God's ways, for they are altogether different from ours. The difference between the two outlooks is the difference between heaven and earth. And so, when something happens which we do not understand, the first thing we have to say to ourselves is, 'Am I facing this spiritually? Am I recollecting that this is a question of my relationship to God? Am I sure my thinking is spiritual at this point? Or have I reverted unconsciously to my natural way of thinking about these things?'

Let me give you a very obvious illustration. I have often known Christian people revert completely from spiritual to rational thinking when talking about politics. On this subject they do not seem to be talking as spiritual people any longer. All the prejudices of the natural person enter in, all the class distinctions, and all the worldly arguments. You would not

imagine from their conversation that they were Christian
people at all. Talk to them about salvation and there is no
doubt about them; but talk about these earthly, worldly
things and they are guilty of all the prejudices of the natural
person, the pride of life and the worldly way of looking at
everything. As Christians we need to be told not to love the
world with its 'lust of the flesh, and the lust of the eyes, and
the pride of life.' Our lives must be consistent. They must be
spiritual at all points; there must be no divergences anywhere.
The Christian must view everything from a spiritual
standpoint.

Spurgeon once told his students that they would find that
people who in prayer meetings prayed like real saints, and
who in general behaved like true saints, in a church meeting
could suddenly become devils. Alas, the history of the church
proves that what he said is but too true. You see, in praying
to God they think spiritually. Then they come to the business
of the church and become devils. Why? Because they start
off in an unspiritual manner, on the assumption that there is
some essential difference between a church meeting and a
prayer meeting. They have a party spirit within them and out
it comes. It is simply because they forget that they need to
think spiritually in everything. The first principle we lay
down, therefore is, that we must learn to think spiritually
always. If we do not, we shall soon find ourselves in this
same dangerous postion which the Psalmist describes so
graphically.

That brings me to the second principle, which is purely
practical. How are we to promote and encourage spiritual
thinking? How can we bring ourselves to think spiritually?
Obviously that is our great need. Well, this man tells us.
'When I thought to know this, it was too painful for me;
until I went into the sanctuary of God; then understood I
their end.' What does it mean? Let me put it like this. We
must learn how to direct ourselves and all our thinking into
the spiritual realm, and it is very clear how this happened in
the Psalmist's case. Let us analyse the psychological process
through which he went. (Incidentally, there is such a thing
as spiritual and biblical psychology, though it is not called
that very frequently.) How did it come about in his case?

I think it happened like this. We have seen that when he was on the point of saying what should never be said, he thought of his fellow-believers. That pulled him up and steadied him, and held him. But fortunately he did not stop at that. 'I have to consider my fellow-believers,' he said. 'But who are they? Where do I meet them? I always meet them in the sanctuary.' So he hastened there. He had been staying away from the sanctuary, as we all tend to do when we get into this kind of difficulty.

The trouble with this man was that his thoughts had been turned in on himself and so had got into a vicious circle. We start thinking about things in this way, we become miserable and unhappy, and we do not want to see anybody. We do not want to mix with God's people. We become preoccupied with our troubles – the hard times we are having, the feeling that God is not fair to us and that we are being treated very harshly. We are miserable and feeling very sorry for ourselves, and there we are, going round and round in circles of self-pity. Self is always at the centre of this problem. The first thing to do, therefore, is to stop this preoccupation with self and to stop turning round and round in circles on the natural level!

But how does one break out of the vicious circle? I suggest that there are three main things here. I would put first what this man puts first – literally going to the house of God. What a wonderful place God's house is. Often you will find deliverance by merely coming into it. Many a time have I thanked God for his house. I thank God that he had ordained that his people should meet together in companies, and worship together. The house of God has delivered me from 'the mumps and measles of the soul' a thousand times and more – merely to enter its doors. How does it work? I think it works like this. The very fact that there is a house of God to come to at all tells us something. How has it come into being? It is God who has planned and arranged it. To realize that in itself puts us immediately into a more healthy condition. Then we begin to go back through history, and remind ourselves of certain truths. Here am I at this present time with this terrible problem, but the Christian church has existed all these long years. (I am already beginning to think in an entirely different way.) The house of God goes back through the centuries to the time of our Lord himself. What is it for? What is its significance? And the cure has begun.

Again, we go to the house of God, and to our amazement we find other people there before us. We are rather surprised at that, because in our private misery and perplexity we had come to the conclusion that perhaps there was nothing in religion at all, and that it was not worth continuing with it. But here are people who think it is worth continuing with; and we feel better. We begin to say: Perhaps I may be wrong; all these people think there is something in it; they may be right. The healing process is going on, the cure is being continued.

Then we go a step farther. We look round the congregation and suddenly find ourselves looking at someone whom we know has had an infinitely worse time than we have been having. We thought our problem was the most terrible problem in the world, and that no-one had ever before suffered as we had. Then we see a poor woman, a widow perhaps, whose only child has died or has been killed. But she is still there. It puts our problem into a new perspective immediately. The great apostle Paul has a word for this, as for all things. 'There hath no temptation taken you,' he reminds us, 'but such as is common to man' (1 Corinthians 10:13). Where the devil gets us is just here. He persuades us that nobody has ever had this trial before: no-one has ever had a problem like mine, no-one else has been dealt with like this. But Paul says, 'There hath no temptation taken you but such as is common to man,' and the moment you remember even that much, you feel better. All God's people know something about this; we are such strange creatures, and sin has had a strange effect upon us. We are always helped in our suffering by hearing that somebody else is suffering too! It is true of us physically, and it is true on the spiritual level also. The realization that we are not alone in this helps to put the thing in the right perspective. I am one of a number; it seems to be something that happens to God's people – the house of God reminds us of all that.

Then it reminds us of things that go still farther back. We begin to study the history of the church throughout the ages, and we remember what we read years ago, perhaps something in the lives of some of the saints. And we begin to understand that some of the greatest saints that have ever adorned the life of the church have experienced trials and troubles and tribulations which cause our little problem to pale into insignificance. The house of God, the sanctuary of God, reminds us of all that. And immediately we are beginning to climb, we are going upwards, we have our problem now in its right setting. The house of God, the sanctuary of the Lord, teaches us all these lessons. People who neglect attendence at the house of God are not only being unscriptural – let me put it bluntly – they are fools. My experience in the ministry has taught me that those who are least regular in their attendance are the ones who are most troubled by problems and perplexities. There is something in the atmosphere of God's house. It is ordained that we should come to God's house to meet his people. It is his ordinance, not ours. He has ordained it not only so that we may meet each other but also that we might come to know him better. Moreover, those who do not attend God's house will be disappointed some day, because on some favoured occasion the Lord will descend in revival and they will not be there. It is a very foolish Christian who does not attend the sanctuary of God as often as he possibly can, and who does not grieve when he cannot.

The second thing that helps us to think spiritually is the Bible. Now in the days of the Psalmist they did not have God's Word as you and I have it today. It is not only in the sanctuary, it is available everywhere. Turn to it in the home or in the church, it does not matter where, and it will immediately make you think spiritually. It does so in countless ways. One of the reasons why God has given us this Word is in order to help us to deal with this problem that we are considering. The mere history in the Bible is invaluable, even if there were nothing else. Take a Psalm like this one and its story. Merely to read what this man went through puts me right, and all the histories do the same. But that is not God's only way of giving this great teaching. Begin to read your Bible and its great teaching and doctrines and you are again reminded of God's gracious purposes for mankind. At once you begin to feel ashamed of your foul thoughts. So in varied ways the same result is produced by the Scriptures.

Then it has explicit teaching on the question of the suffering of the godly. Paul writes to Timothy, who was ready to whimper and complain when things went wrong, and he says to him, 'Yea, and all that will live godly in Christ Jesus shall suffer persecution' (2 Timothy 3:12). Timothy could not understand it. He was afraid because he saw that the servants of God were being persecuted, and many a servant of God has felt the same since. Again, Paul speaking to the early Christian churches told them that it is 'through much tribulation' that we must enter into the kingdom of God. If we grasp Paul's teaching to the early Christian churches we shall not be surprised at the things that happen to us. Indeed, instead of being surprised at them we almost get to the stage in which we expect them, in which we feel like saying: If I am not having troubles, what is wrong with me? Why are things going so well with me? In other words, the whole atmosphere of the Bible is spiritual, and the more we read it, the more we shall be delivered from the rational level and raised to that higher level where we see things on the spiritual plane.

Just a word on the other essential aid – prayer and meditation. That is what goes on in the sanctuary of God. The Psalmist did not merely go to the building, he went to meet God. The sanctuary is the place in which God's honour dwells, the meeting-place for God and his people. It is when we come face to face with God and meditate upon him that we are finally delivered from that low level of rational thinking and begin again to think spiritually. I wonder whether there is someone who is surprised that I have not put prayer first, or at least before this. I am sure there are some, because I know a number of Christian people who have a universal answer to all questions. It does not matter what the question is, they always say, 'Pray about it.' If someone in the Psalmist's condition had come to any one of them they would have said, 'Go and pray about it.' What a glib, superficial and false bit of advice that can often be, and I am saying that from a Christian pulpit. You may ask, Is it ever wrong to tell people to make their problems a matter of prayer? It is never wrong, but it is sometimes quite futile.

What I mean is this. The whole trouble with this poor man, in a sense, was that he was so muddled in his thinking about God that he could not pray to him. If we have muddled thoughts in our mind and heart concerning God's way with respect to us, how can we pray? We cannot. Before we can pray truly we must think spiritually. There is nothing more fatuous than glib talk about prayer, as if prayer were something which you can always immediately rush into.

In case you doubt my word, let me quote one of the greatest heroes of prayer the world has ever known. I refer to the great George Müller of Bristol. George Müller, in lecturing to ministers, in particular, on this question of prayer, told them this. He said that for many years the first thing he did every morning of his life was to pray. He had now long since discovered that that was not the best way. He had found that in order to pray truly and spiritually, he had to be in the Spirit himself, and that he must prepare himself first. He had discovered that it was good and most helpful, and he now strongly recommended it to them, always to read a portion of Scripture and perhaps some devotional book before they began to pray. In other words, he found it was necessary to put himself and his spirit right, before he could truly pray to God.

Now that is exactly what happened to this Psalmist. He was in a vicious circle and, thinking as he did, he could not pray because his whole thinking was wrong. Now in the steps I have enumerated his thinking was put right, and then he was in the right condition to pray. Very often we waste our time thinking we are praying when we are not really praying at all. Often it is only some sort of crying out in desperation. Our whole mind is wrong and so is our attitude, and we cannot pray like that. We must take time with prayer. We do not begin to pray to God until we realize his presence, and we do not realize his presence until our thinking about him is right. Paul said again to the Philippians, 'We are the circumcision, which worship God in the spirit, and rejoice in Christ Jesus, and have no confidence in the flesh' (Philippians 3:3). We must pray 'in the Spirit'. We must be spiritually prepared, and that means that our thinking is straight and true. So the steps are perfectly right – the house of God, the Word of

God, prayer to God and communion with God. Thus, having realized that all those other thoughts were blasphemous and wrong, when our spirit is cleansed and bathed, we turn to God and we face him, and our spirit finds rest. That is the process, or, rather, that is the beginning. We have not finished yet, but having got a foothold, that is how the process continues. In trouble, 'until I went into the sanctuary of God' – and found myself face to face with him.

Chapter Four

FACING ALL THE FACTS

When I thought to know this,
it was too painful for me;
Until I went into the sanctuary of God;
then understood I their end.

We must now go on, because the Psalmist's process of recovery did not stop with his going to the sanctuary. That step is vital, and I must again emphasize it. But it is not enough. This man went into the sanctuary of God and that alone put his thinking in the right atmosphere. But he went beyond that. What happened to him in the sanctuary? He tells us. 'When I thought to know this, it was too painful for me; until I went into the sanctuary of God; then understood I their end.'

The first word we have to deal with is this word 'understood'. This is, again, one of those great fundamental principles of our faith which we can so easily forget. What we find in the sanctuary of God is not merely a general influence, not merely a matter of atmosphere. When this man went into the sanctuary of God he was given *understanding*. He did not merely feel better; he was put right in his thinking. He did not merely forget his problem for the time being; he found a solution.

I wonder how this can be put plainly and clearly. It is such a vital point. Religion should not act as a drug on us. There are people in whose case it does act like that. It may be a terrible thing to say, but to be honest I have to say it. There is often, far too often, justification for the charge that religion is nothing but 'the opiate of the people'. To many people it is a form of dope and nothing else, and their idea of the house of God and worship is just of a place where they can forget their troubles for the time being. That is why they may be interested in the aesthetic aspect – a beautiful service in a beautiful setting. They are not interested in an exposition of the Truth – hence their preference for very short sermons. They are only interested in some general soothing effect, and while they are in the service they forget their troubles. 'How nice, how beautiful!' they say. But that is not the religion of the Bible. 'Then understood I their end.' What happened to this man was not that he went to the Temple – into the church, so to speak – and that, listening to the strains of beautiful music coming from the organ, and looking at the stained-glass windows and the beautiful lighting, he gradually began to feel a little bit better and forgot his troubles for the time being. No! It was something rational – 'then understood I their end' – it was a matter of understanding.

True religion was never meant just to produce some general effect. The Bible is a revelation of God's ways with respect to mankind. It is meant to give 'understanding'. If our practice of religion does not give us understanding, then it is something that may well do us harm and we should be better without it. I am sure that I need not stress the vital importance of this. There are many things that we could do that would make us feel better temporarily. There are many ways of forgetting our troubles for a while. Some go to the cinema, others run to the public-house or to the bottle of whisky which they keep at home. Under its effect and influence they feel much better and happier; their problem does not seem so acute. Others run to the cults, such as Christian Science, which is rubbish philosophically, but often makes people 'feel better'. There are many ways of giving temporary relief, but the question is, Do they give understanding, do they really help us to see through our trouble?

Now that sort of false comfort can be given in the house of God. There are people who seem to think that the right thing to do in the house of God is just to go on singing choruses and a certain type of hymn until you are almost in a state of intoxication. Indeed, the whole service is with a view to 'conditioning'. You come under some emotional influence and you do feel better. The world does that. It makes people sing comic songs to appropriate music, and they are wafted under its influence into a state in which they definitely, for the moment, feel better. All that may be of the very devil, because the test of the value of these things is not whether it makes me feel better or not, but whether it gives me understanding. 'Then understood I.'

Let us never forget that the message of the Bible is addressed primarily to the mind, to the understanding. There is nothing about the gospel that is more satisfying than this. It does not merely give me an experience; it enables me to understand life. I have knowledge; I have understanding; I know. I can 'give a reason' for the hope that is in me. I do not merely say that 'whereas I was blind, now I see', without knowing why or how. I know; I can give reasons for the hope that is in me. Thank God that this man when he went into the sanctuary of God found an explanation. It was not merely some temporary relief that he received; it was not some kind of injection that was given to him to assuage the pain just a little for the moment, not a treatment which would leave the problem still there, so that when he got home and the effect had passed he would be back again where he was before. Not at all. Having started to think straight in the Temple of God he went home and continued to think straight. And it ended in the production of this Psalm!

Understanding! Do you know in whom you have believed? Do you know what you believe? Are you interested in Christian doctrine? What is your chief desire? Is it simply to be happy or is it to know the truth? It is one of the most searching questions that can ever be put to Christian people. God forbid that we should ever be people who are simply out for entertainment, and whose religious services cater for that. I speak advisedly, because there is a very real risk of this. I once had to speak in a very famous Bible Conference. I was there for four days and every service was introduced by forty minutes of music of varied types. I did not hear the Scriptures read once during the entire time of that Bible Conference. A friend of mind had a similar experience in a famous church in a certain continent. A number of people were being dedicated for the mission field that morning and there was also a Communion service. There were two anthems by the choir, three solos and a very brief prayer. But the Scriptures were not read at all. And that church has a very great reputation as an evangelical church. You do not get understanding that way – by having a musical entertainment and cutting down the reading and exposition of the Scriptures. That is a travesty of the biblical picture of a church. 'Then understood I.' It is because so many do not understand that they are always grumbling and complaining; and it is also the reason why so many do not have any real insight into the times through which we are passing.

Very well, that is the first thing that going into the sanctuary did for the Psalmist. It gave him understanding, it put him on his feet. But we must take that farther. How was he given understanding? The answer is that what happened to him in the sanctuary taught him how to think aright. In other words, not only must our thinking be put right in its very atmosphere, not only must it become spiritual instead of being merely rational; there must be a correction in detail also. That is what happened to this man.

Let us divide it up like this. He tells us that in the first place certain general defects in his thinking were corrected, and then he goes on to tell us how certain detailed aspects of his thinking were put right. For the moment we shall deal mainly with the general. Here the first thing that is necessary is that our thinking should be whole and not partial. This man's fall had been arrested, but he was still unhappy. He was in agony of mind until he went into the sanctuary of God. 'Then understood I their end.' Here is the thing he had forgotten! His thinking, he saw, had been incomplete.

I suppose, in the last analysis, that one of our central troubles is that our thinking tends to be partial and incomplete. You remember that line of Matthew Arnold's, 'Who saw life steadily, and saw it whole.' You cannot pay anyone a greater compliment than to say that he saw life steadily and that he saw it whole. I think it was the late Earl of Oxford and Asquith who once said that the greatest gift someone could ever have was the capacity for what he called 'cubical' thinking, the ability to see all sides of a subject. Truth is like a cube, and you must see all the facets. The failure to do that, I think you will find as we analyse ourselves, is the trouble with most of us. Take the Psalmist, for instance. It was obviously the root of all his trouble. He was just looking at one side, and he saw nothing else, and it gripped and held him. What happened when he went into the sanctuary of God? He began to see the other sides. He began to see things as a whole instead of merely in part.

Is that not the whole trouble with prejudice? We are all born into this world as creatures of prejudice; and most errors are ultimately to be explained in terms of prejudice. Prejudice is a power that pre-judges issues, and it does it by shutting out all aspects of truth except one. It will not allow you to see the others. People who are guilty of prejudice invariably betray the source of their trouble. They say, 'I have always said this.' Exactly. They will not see any other side. Prejudice holds you to the one facet and it will never allow you to move. The result is that you are blind to every other side. This accounts for much of the tragedy of the world, and certainly for most of our errors.

Now I would suggest that anyone who is not a Christian is really in that position, because he does not see the whole situation. It is the thing that explains unbelief, it is the thing that explains most of the mistakes people make in life. Take, for instance, materialism. The philosphy of materialism is not as popular as it used to be. Towards the end of the last century it was the controlling philosophy; everything was explained in terms of it. It is no longer popular, because the new nuclear physics is really smashing the whole materialistic philosophy, for it tells us that even material objects are full of movement and power. Nothing is static or inert. There are forces, mighty forces everywhere, and what we call matter is nothing but mighty atomic energy holding certain things together. If you had said this in the early years of this century it would have been regarded as scientific blasphemy. The materialistic outlook was in control. Why? They were only looking at one side, they did not know all the facts. Now the materialistic view of matter has had to go.

I can illustrate the same thing in the realm of medicine.

The thing to do in medicine today – and let me remind you that there are fashions even in medicine – is to talk about psychosomatic medicine. At long last the medical profession has discovered that the patient himself is important. Until recently their interest seemed to be in disease or in particular parts of a person's body, while the patient himself was ignored. Someone went to a doctor and the doctor was interested only in the pains in his stomach. And they explained the pains in the stomach as due, so they thought, to local conditions in the stomach – acidity, *etc.* In my student days, if I had been asked the commonest cause of pains in the stomach and had said, 'Worry and anxiety,' they would have thought there was something wrong with me, and would have dismissed my answer as being unscientific. But by today they have discovered that that is really the answer. A person's body and its functioning is not merely a physical matter, his mind also is important in the context of his health. Anxiety, worry, all these things cause messages to be sent from the mind to the local parts of the body. The body is not only matter and material. Today, the importance of the mind is realized, although as yet the spiritual element or factor is still not recognized. God grant that they may come soon to see that the spirit is as important as the psyche.

In the same way I could show you that the whole idea of mankind as an economic unit is based upon the same fallacy. The trouble is that they only see one aspect. When they say that that is everything, they are simply prejudiced and have forgotten the other facts which are equally important. To people who believe in economics the whole problem of mankind is one of economics. No, says someone else, not economics but biology, and he in turn is ready to suggest that the entire person and all his behaviour can be explained in terms of the balance of his ductless glands.

Others say that all this is quite wrong, and that we are essentially intellectual. They seem to think of mankind as pure intellect sitting in a vacuum, entirely rational, with no other factors in its make-up! We will not elaborate further, but is it not obvious that the trouble with all these theories is that they are looking at only one side, one aspect, and so their solutions are partial and incomplete? What they are forgetting, and what so many others are forgetting, is life itself. They are forgetting the sensibilities, and such factors as emotion. These things are left out, and yet they are all a part of life; indeed, they are central. Lusts, desires, sin, evil, all these things come into the picture, all these facts make us what we are and make life what it is. 'There are more things in heaven and earth, Horatio, than are dreamt of in your philosophy.' That is what we should say to the modern person. That is how Shakespeare put it. I am not sure that Browning did not say it even better. You remember the great poem, *Bishop Blougram's Apology?* You remember the interview between the old Bishop and the young journalist who had become dissatisfied with the Christian religion? The young man was going to think life right through. He was going to break with everything he had been taught in the past, he was going to think things through for himself and make a new philosophy. The old Bishop said, in effect: Do you know, I was once a young man and I did exactly the same thing. I thought I had a perfect understanding, I assembled all the component parts, I had a complete scheme and philosophy of life, I thought nothing could upset it, but – 'Just when we're safest, there's a sunset-touch'. Just when we think, to use the modern jargon, we have the whole of life 'taped', just when we think our philosophy is perfect,

> *Just when we're safest, there's a sunset-touch,*
> *A fancy from a flower-bell, some one's death,*
> *A chorus-ending from Euripides,*
> *And that's enough for fifty hopes and fears, –*
> *The grand Perhaps.*

You see what Browning means. With our rational mind we draw up our plan of life and think we can explain everything and that we have catered for everything. But just when we have done so, we take, perhaps, a walk in the country – we see a sunset, a glorious, golden sunset that moves us to the very depth of our being, in a manner we cannot explain. Or it may be 'A fancy from a flower-bell' or 'someone's death'. Our philosophy somehow does not cover it, or explain it. There is a mystery about it which we cannot fathom. 'The grand Perhaps'! There is something else after all, beyond, above, behind all we can understand.

> *And that's enough for fifty hopes and fears, –*
> *The grand Perhaps.*

Or, as Tennyson put it:

> *Our little systems have their day;*
> *They have their day and cease to be:*
> *They are but broken lights of thee,*
> *And thou, O Lord, art more than they.*

That is what a person sees when he comes into the sanctuary of God. He begins to see things as a whole, he is reminded of things he had forgotten and ignored. The apostle Paul put this in a marvellous phrase. There was a time when he hated the name of Jesus of Nazareth and he persecuted his people. He thought he was doing God service by killing Christian people. But when he saw him and came to know him, everything became new, and looking back on his old life he said, 'I verily thought with myself, that I ought to do many things contrary to the name of Jesus of Nazareth' (Acts 26:9). Precisely. He thought 'with himself', instead of thinking with Christ. It was prejudice. 'I thought with myself.' As long as you and I think with ourselves we shall never see life truly.

Is not this the whole trouble with life today? I read a book which was designed to tell us how life should be ordered and run in this country. It is a very able book; the argument, I felt, was most convincing. The scheme for the social and economic running of this country seemed perfect. But there was one defect; the man who wrote it did not know anything about the doctrine of sin. If everybody in this country had been perfect that scheme would have been perfect. But the author forgot that men and women do not live by ideals but by desires, that we are governed by what we want and what we like. We have passions and lusts. We are creatures of greed and envy, of thirst and sensuality. These things are in our very constitutions. Mankind itself had been forgotten in that book; and that is the ultimate fallacy and the cause of the failure of every idealist system ever proposed by us. You can plan to abolish war and to make a permanent state of peace in this world. Such plans are all perfect in theory, but they forget greed, they forget desire, they forget these failings that are in human nature, even in the very mind of mankind. You may produce a perfect scheme, then someone – perhaps some member of the very group or conference planning the scheme – will suddenly desire something, and your perfect scheme comes to nothing.

We must face all the facts. 'Then understood I their end.' There were facts that he had not considered, there were elements he had not taken in. Take in all the facts; think as a whole; think of yourself as a whole. Realize the corruptness of your own human nature. Realize also that you are not merely a body. There are other factors in life, and unless you have considered them you do not know life truly. These other things matter. Lift up your eyes on the 'mysterious universe' and try to explain it. See how you fit into it. See its mystery and marvel. Can you reduce it all to the material level only? Of course you cannot; the scientist himself cannot. Or, take a book on history. See how history works, observe its processes. Can you really explain the whole of history in terms of evolution? Face the facts. Oh, the folly of the person who says that humanity is automatically getting better and better! Can you say, in the light of the things we are constantly reading in the newspapers, that the human race is on the way to perfection, that it is better than it was? Read history, look at it as a whole, and you will see that our race still behaves as mankind in sin has always done.

Now look at Christ. Look at his life, look at the record of what he has done. Stand before the cross, face it and try to explain it. Then look at the story of the church and the martyrs and the saints. Take it all in. Do not be content with anything less than all. Then rise to the ultimate height, and stand before God. Lack of true thinking is our ultimate trouble, for if we do not think of all the aspects and phases, if we do not face all the facts, we shall inevitably go astray. If, therefore, you feel that you have a grudge against life and against God and you are feeling sorry for yourself, I have but one word to say to you. Hasten to the sanctuary; consider all the facts; remember the things you have forgotten.

There is, however, one further principle. Not only did this man see that his thinking had not taken all the facts into consideration, he saw in addition that he had not been thinking things right through to the end. Many of the troubles in life today are due to the fact that people still fail to think things right through. This man looked only at the prosperity of the ungodly. But when he went into the sanctuary of God, at once he could say, 'Then understood I their end.'

That is a great theme in the Bible. James has a great word to say about the case of Job. He says, 'Ye have heard of the patience of Job, and have seen the end of the Lord' (James 5:11). Job had been having a hard time, and he could not understand what was the matter. He had not thought on to 'the end' of the Lord. The end of the story in the last chapter of Job is that Job, who had been bereft of everything, ended by having much more than he had before. That is 'the end' of the Lord. Go on to the end. Do not stop short. Is that not the argument of Psalm 37? What the Psalmist says there is that he had seen the wicked in great power and spreading himself like a green bay-tree, but when the end came he had vanished off the face of the earth, and no-one could find him. So he says, 'Mark the perfect man, and behold the upright: for the end of that man is peace' (verse 37). The importance of 'the end' is something which is constantly emphasized in the Bible.

Our Lord has put it once and for ever in the Sermon on the Mount. 'Enter ye in at the strait gate: for wide is the gate, and broad is the way, that leadeth to destruction, and many there be which go in thereat: because strait is the gate, and narrow is the way, which leadeth unto life, and few there be that find it.' You see what he is saying. Look at the broad way, how marvellous it seems. You can go in with the crowd, you can do what everybody else is doing, and they are all smiling and joking. Wide and broad are the gate and the way. It all seems so marvellous. And this other seems so miserable – 'strait is the gate'. One at a time, a personal decision, fighting self, taking up the cross. 'Strait is the gate, and narrow is the way.' And it is because they look only at the beginning that so many people are on the broad way. What is the matter with them? They do not look at the end. 'Wide is the gate, and broad is the way, that leadeth to destruction.' 'Strait is the gate, and narrow is the way', but – and that is the end – it 'leadeth unto life'.

The end of the one is destruction, of the other, life. The trouble in life today is that people look only at the beginning. Their view of life is what we may call the cinema or film-star view of life. It always attracts, and all those who live that life are apparently having a marvellous time. Alas that so many young people are brought up to think that that is life, and that always to live like that must be supreme happiness. But look at the end of those people. Look at them passing in and out of the divorce courts as they turn marriage into licensed prostitution, unworthy to have children because of their selfishness and because they do not know how to bring them up. But people are attracted by the appearance. They look only at the surface; they look only at the beginning. They do not look at this type of life in its end; they give no thought whatsoever to the ultimate outcome. Nevertheless, it is as true today as it has ever been, and the Bible has always said it, that the end of these things is 'destruction'.

There is nothing so hopeless in the world, ultimately, as the bankruptcy of the non-Christian view of life. Do you know that Charles Darwin, the author of *The Origin of Species*, confessed at the end of his life that, as a result of concentrating on one aspect only of life, he had lost the power to enjoy poetry and music, and to a large extent, even the power to appreciate nature itself. Poor Charles Darwin. Whereas he used to enjoy poetry when he was a young man, now alas in his old age he found no pleasure in it, and music came to mean nothing to him. He had concentrated so much on the details of one area in life that he had deliberately circumscribed his field of vision instead of allowing the glorious panorama of the whole to speak to him. The end of H. G. Wells was very similar. He who had claimed so much for the mind and human understanding, and who had ridiculed Christianity with its doctrines of sin and salvation, at the end of his life confessed that he was utterly baffled and bewildered. The very title of his last book – *Mind at the End of its Tether* – bears eloquent testimony to the Bible's teaching about the tragedy of the end of the ungodly. Or take the phrase from the autobiography of a rationalist such as Dr Marrett who was the head of a college in Oxford. He writes

123

like this: 'But to me the war brought to a sudden end the long summer of my life. Henceforth I have nothing to look forward to but chill autumn and still chillier winter, and yet I must somehow try not to lose heart.' The death of the ungodly is a terrible thing. Read their biographies. Their glittering days are at an end. What have they now? They have nothing to look forward to, and, like the late Lord Simon, try to comfort themselves by reliving their former successes and triumphs. Such is the end of the ungodly.

Contrast that with the godly life, which on the surface seems at first so narrow and miserable. Even a hireling prophet such as Balaam, bad man as he was, understood something about that. 'Let me die the death of the righteous, and let my last end be like his!' said he. In other words, 'I have to say this, these godly people know how to die; I wish I could die like them.' In the book of Proverbs we read that 'the way of the wicked is as darkness'. 'But the path of the just is as the shining light, that shineth more and more unto the perfect day' (Proverbs 4:19, 18). What a glory! Let us come back to Psalm 37, 'Mark the perfect man, and behold the upright: for the end of that man is peace.' And then listen to the apostle Paul. In spite of all his tribulations and persecutions, his trials and disappointments, listen to him as he faces the end, 'I am now ready to be offered, and the time of my departure is at hand. I have fought a good fight, I have finished my course, I have kept the faith: henceforth there is laid up for me a crown of righteousness, which the Lord, the righteous judge, shall give me at that day: and [thank God for this] not to me only, but unto all them also that love his appearing' (2 Timothy 4:6–8). That is the way to die, that is the way to end. One of John Wesley's proudest claims for his early Methodists was, 'Our people die well.'

The Bible everywhere urges us to consider our 'latter end'. Do not go to church merely to consider your present prospects; consider your latter end. 'The end.' How glorious it would be for all of us to be able to face it as the apostle Paul did, and to be able to say, 'Henceforth there is laid up for me a crown of righteousness, which the Lord, the righteous judge, shall give me at that day.' The way to be able to say that, and to be certain that you will receive that crown, is first to look at the two possibilities as a whole, and having done so, to go immediately to God and confess your blindness, your prejudice, your folly in trusting to your own understanding, and then to ask him to receive you. Tell him you accept his message concerning Jesus Christ his only begotten Son, who came into the world to die for your sins and to deliver you. Yield yourself to him and rely upon him and his power. Give yourself unreservedly to him in Christ and you will see life with a wholeness and a blessedness you have never known before. And the end will be glorious. Your path will be as the shining light that shineth more and more, however black the world may become and, even in the shadow of death, it will shine more and more unto the perfect day. 'Then understood I their end.'

Chapter Five

BEGINNING TO UNDERSTAND

Surely thou didst set them in slippery
  places:
thou castedst them down into destruction.
How are they brought into desolation, as
  in a moment!
they are utterly consumed with terrors.
As a dream when one awaketh;
so, O Lord, when thou awakest,
thou shalt despise their image.

We have reached the point at which we have seen the Psalmist's thinking put right in general. We proceed now to consider how it was also put right in certain particular respects.

As we saw in the previous chapter, he discovered that his thinking about the ungodly had been most defective. Here he was in the Temple. But what was the origin of the Temple? That question made him consider the whole history of God's people and all the enemies and opposition they had had to encounter and to overcome. And always the story was that God had delivered his people and routed their enemies. The history of the Christian church should do the same for us. Lord Macaulay once said, 'No man who is correctly informed as to the past will be disposed to take a morose or desponding view of the present.' If that is true in general, it is particularly true in the realm of the Christian faith. It is our ignorance of

127

church history, and particularly of the history recorded in the Bible, that so frequently causes us to stumble and to despair.

What, then, is the teaching of the Bible in this respect? The first thing we find is that it gives us actual history. We cannot remind ourselves too frequently of stories such as those of the Flood, of Sodom and Gomorrah, the Philistines, Assyrians, Babylonians and Belshazzar. They all teach the same lesson, of God's triumph over his enemies. But towering above them all is the great fact of the resurrection which shows God triumphing finally over the devil and all his powers. The continuing victory is seen everywhere in the Acts of the Apostles, and a grand view of the end is given in the book of Revelation.

The actual history of the Christian church since the days of the apostles continues the same story. We know what has happened to all powers such as the Jews, Romans, *etc.*, that have attempted to exterminate the Christian church. We also know the epic stories of the martyrs and early confessors, the Waldensian Church, the early Protestants, the Puritans and the Covenanters. Indeed, this very century in which we live has provided us with yet further evidence.

The Bible, however, does not merely record history. It helps us to understand the meaning of history. It teaches certain principles very clearly. The first is that all things, even the evil powers, are under God's hand. As the Psalmist puts it here in verse 18, 'Surely thou didst set them in slippery places.' They are not free agents. Nothing happens apart from God. 'The Lord reigneth.' 'By me kings reign.' It is of vital importance that we should grasp the biblical doctrine of Providence. It can be defined as, 'That continued exercise of the divine energy whereby the Creator upholds all his creatures, is operative in all that transpires in the world, and directs all things to their appointed end.' God is over all, and as we read in Psalm 76:10, 'Surely the wrath of man shall praise thee: the remainder of wrath shalt thou restrain.' In connection with this we have to remember God's permissive will. It is beyond our understanding, but it is clearly taught that he permits certain things to happen for his own purposes.

Another thing we see clearly here is that the whole position of the ungodly is precarious and dangerous. They are in 'slippery places'. All they have is but temporary. The Psalmist suddenly saw clearly what Moses saw when he chose 'rather to suffer affliction with the people of God, than to enjoy the pleasures of sin for a season'. Age and decay, death and judgment, are certain. The most terrible thing about sin is that it blinds people to the realization of this. They do not see that their pomp and glory are but for a season. 'The Lord reigneth; let the people tremble.'

The Psalmist saw this so clearly in the sanctuary of God that he not only ceased to be envious of the ungodly, but we get the impression that he even began to feel sorry for them as he realized the truth about their position. Thus, his thinking with respect to the ungodly was put right, and there is perhaps no better test of our own profession of the Christian faith than just this. Do we feel sorry for the ungodly in their blindness? Have we even a sense of compassion for them as we see them as sheep without a shepherd?

We proceed now to consider the next step and to show how this man's thinking was put right also about God himself. We have seen how his thinking about God had gone seriously wrong because he had started in the wrong way about the ungodly, and thus had got into the position of questioning and querying even God. He says, 'Verily I have cleansed my heart in vain, and washed my hands in innocency.' In other words, 'I have been trying to obey God, but it does not really seem to pay. Is God what he says he is?' Now that is a terrible thing to think; and that is, particularly, the thing on which we must now concentrate. This man shows us how his thinking about God was put right. In a sense he has already said it, 'Surely thou didst set them in slippery places.' The moment he utters that word *thou* one feels that the whole position is beginning to change.

What was it that was adjusted when he began thinking truly about God? I think the first thing was his attitude to the character of God; because, after all, what this man had been beginning to doubt was the very character of God himself. Many of these Psalmists with strange and remarkable honesty confess that they were tempted along that line. For instance, in Psalm 77 the same thing is clearly expressed. The Psalmist asks, 'Will the Lord cast off for ever? and will he be favourable no more? Is his mercy clean gone for ever? doth his promise fail for evermore? Hath God forgotten to be gracious? . . .' That is the type of question they were asking, and, as I pointed out at the very beginning, some of the greatest saints have sometimes been tempted to ask these questions when things have gone against them. Well, this man in the same way had been asking these same questions: Does God care, and if he does care why does he not stop these things? Is it that he cannot? And so doubts about the character of God lead to doubts about his power.

How often people have asked these questions! How often did people say in the last world war: Why does God permit a man like Hitler to live? If he is God and is all-powerful why doesn't he strike him down? The question then suggests itself: Is God perhaps unable to do it? Or: Have we been mistaken in our ideas about God? Have we been wrong in our ideas about his mercy and compassion and goodness? Why does he not demolish these people who are opposed to him and his people? Those are the questions that tend to agitate our minds in times of trial.

Now this man had been assailed by just such questions; and here, now, he finds his answer. At once he is put right by remembering the greatness and the power of God – '*thou didst set them in slippery places*'. There is nothing outside the control of God. Many of the Psalms express this, as for example Psalm 50. It is, indeed, one of the great themes of the Bible. There is no limit to the power of God. He is eternal in all his powers and in all his attributes. 'He spake, and it was done.' He created everything out of nothing; he suspends the universe in space. Read certain great chapters of the book of Job (chapter 28, for example) and you will find it expressed in a most amazing manner.

'In the beginning God.' This is a fundamental postulate; the Bible asserts it everywhere. Whatever the explanation may be of all that is happening in the world, it is not that God is not capable of stopping it. It is not that he cannot arrest these things, because the power of God, by definition, is illimitable. He is absolute; he is the everlasting, eternal God to whom everything on earth is but as nothing. He owns everything;

he governs, he controls everything; all things are under his hands. 'The Lord reigneth.' Now that is the first thing about which this man was put right, and that very clearly.

But, in the second place, he was also put right on the question of the righteousness and justice of God. That is the order in which these things arise. If God has the power, why does he not exercise it? If God has the ability to destroy all his enemies, why does he allow them to do the things they do? Why are the ungodly allowed to flourish? What about the justice and righteousness of God? The answer is given in the words of Abraham of old, 'Shall not the Judge of all the earth do right?' (Genesis 18:25). It is as fundamental a postu-late as that concerning the greatness and the might and the majesty of God. God is eternally just and right. God cannot change. God cannot (I say it with reverence, it is a part of the truth concerning the holiness of God) – God cannot be unjust. It is impossible.

James puts it like this: 'Let no man say when he is tempted, I am tempted of God: for God cannot be tempted with evil, neither tempteth he any man.' He is 'the Father of lights, with whom is no variableness, neither shadow of turning' (James 1:13, 17). If it were possible for any change or modific-ation to take place in God he would no longer be God. God, as he has revealed to us about himself, is, from everlasting to everlasting, always, ever the same; never any difference, never any modification. So Abraham is obviously right when he says, 'Shall not the Judge of all the earth do right?' He can do no other. We must realize this, so that, when we are tempted of the devil, or by our own predicament, or by any position which the devil may use, to query the righteousness of God, we may understand that what we are really doing is to imply that it is possible for God to vary and to change. But that is impossible. He cannot, because God is God, and, because of what he is, there can never be any variation in his justice or righteousness, there can never be any question of injustice or unrighteousness.

But we must go beyond that. The Psalmist went beyond that and came to the point at which he discovered that the covenant of God, and the promises of God, are ever faithful and ever sure. In other words, God is not only just and right, but God has committed himself to mankind. He has given certain promises. Therefore the next great doctrine of the Bible is that the promises of God are always certain and sure; what he has promised, he will most surely and certainly perform. You will remember Paul's word to Titus; he refers to 'God, that cannot lie' (Titus 1:2). And he cannot lie, again for the same reason that God is God. When God gives a promise, that promise is certain to be kept. All his promises are absolute promises, and whatever he has said, he is certainly going to do:

> *For his mercies ay endure,*
> *Ever faithful, ever sure.*

Now that was all-important to this Psalmist, because as one of God's people he knew about the covenant. He knew the promises God had made to his people, and how he had pledged himself to them. He had told them that they were his special, his 'peculiar' people and that he would take a particular interest in them, that he loved them and was concerned about their prosperity and happiness, and that he was going to watch over them and bless them until eventually he received them to himself.

The Psalmist, as we have seen, had been tempted to ask, 'If that is so, why am I like this?' But now in the sanctuary of God he finds that his attitude was wrong, and he sees that God works indirectly as well as directly. It was in the sanctuary of God that he saw that. If you read the verses that follow you will find how he elaborates it all. He says, 'Nevertheless I am continually with thee: thou hast holden me by my right hand. Thou shalt guide me with thy counsel, and afterward receive me to glory.' He sees it all, and so clearly that when he came to write his Psalm he began by saying, 'Truly God is good to Israel' – even when every appearance is to the contrary, God is always good to Israel, he never breaks a promise. These are what we must always regard as fundamental postulates in all our relationships to God, and we must never be tempted to question or query anything along that particular line.

So we see the Psalmist was put right in his thinking about God, first of all with regard to the character of God. We are still confronted, however, by our main question. If I now know that God has all power and that nothing can limit it, that he is always just and righteous, that he is always faithful to his covenant and promises, I therefore ask: Why then is it that the ungodly are allowed to flourish and prosper in this way, and why is it that the godly are so frequently to be found in a state of suffering? Here is the very heart of the question which has always troubled mankind and which is probably being asked by millions of people in different parts of the world at this moment: Why does God permit this kind of thing?

The Psalmist discovered the answer in the house of God. He puts it in a very interesting manner. You will find the same answer in several Psalms, and, indeed, in many other places in the Scriptures. Here it is given in words which we may describe as a very daring anthropomorphism. The Psalmist says that the explanation is that God for the time being seems to be asleep. 'When thou awakest, thou shalt despise their image,' he says in verse 20. Now that is an anthropomorphism. In other words, the Psalmist, in order to convey what he had discovered in the sanctuary of God, has to put it in human terms. Because of the limitations of our thinking and of our language, he uses a pictorial representation in terms of what is true of us as human beings. God cannot sleep; but he appears to be as one sleeping. It is not that he has not the power, but he is for the time being asleep. It is not that he has forgotten to be gracious, he is asleep. That is the argument.

A similar statement is found in the next Psalm in verse 22, where, having described the desolation of the church and the way in which the enemy has come in and has reduced it almost to a shambles, the Psalmist ends with a prayer. He says, 'Arise, O God, plead thine own cause. . . .' It seems as if he turns to God and says, 'God, why don't you awake? Arise, O God. . . .' It is the same idea. In Psalm 44:23 it is even more explicit: 'Awake, why sleepest thou, O Lord? arise, cast us not off for ever.' Here is a man in desperation. He sees the desolation produced by the enemy; he sees the success of the ungodly and the suffering of the godly. He knows that God is just and all-powerful, so, turning to God, he says, 'Awake, why sleepest thou, O Lord?' Why do you not assert yourself? These all express the same idea, and that is the idea which we must now examine in detail.

Why does God thus appear to be asleep? Before I come to the spiritual answer to this question, may I digress for a moment – to indicate the gross inconsistency that is to be found in the argument of people who glibly question God's character and power. There are so many who say: If God is God, and if God has the power, and if God is merciful and gracious, why did he not destroy a man like Hitler at the beginning of his régime; why did he not wipe him out, and all his forces, and thereby save suffering; why did he not intervene earlier; why did he not assert himself? That is the argument they put forward, and yet these are generally the very self-same people who are loudest in their claim for what they call the free will of man. If you begin to preach to them about the doctrines of grace, if you should mention such terms as 'predestination' and 'the elect', they are the first to say, 'I maintain I have a free will; I have a right to do what I like with my own life.' Yet these are the people who say God should exert his power and his might over other people. We cannot have it both ways. If we want God to assert himself in certain things, he must do it in all things, not just in what we choose. There is an utter inconsistency in the argument. When such people are thinking about others they expect God to control them; but when they think of them-selves they say, 'It is very wrong of God to control me. I am a free person; I must be allowed to do whatever I like; I am a free person, I must have my liberty.' Yes, they must have liberty, but the other person must not!

More seriously, why is it, do you think, that God does appear to be asleep? Why is it that he does allow the ungodly to flourish in this way? There are certain very definite answers in the Scriptures to that question. First, there is no doubt at all that one of the reasons is that God permits these things in order that sin may be revealed for what it really is, that he may allow it to manifest itself and show itself in all its ugliness. If you want a classic statement of that you will find it in the second half of Romans 1 where Paul traces the decline and fall in the history of mankind. Paul was writing about the civilization, or society, of his own day. He describes the terrible ugliness and foulness of life, he gives us that horrible list of sins, the sexual perversions and all the other things that characterized life at that time. And he says that the real explanation of it all is that mankind, having substituted the creature for the Creator, and having rebelled against God's holy law, has been given over by God to a reprobate mind. God has withdrawn his restraining power. He has allowed sin to develop and reveal itself for what it really is.

Surely that is something of which we need to be reminded today. There is a great deal of attention being paid at this moment to the moral condition of this country, and very rightly so. Why is this necessary? I suggest the answer is still precisely the same. Our fathers and forefathers increasingly turned their backs upon God. They queried the authority of the Scriptures – it was done even in pulpits – and mankind became the authority. What we think about the Bible, what we think about God, what we think about morality, became the rule. Mankind put itself in the position of authority and turned down the authority of God; and we today are reaping the consequences of that. God, as it were, turns to mankind and says, 'Very well; I will just allow you to see what your views and your philosophies lead to.' Today we are beginning to see what sin really is. It is revealing itself in its ugliness. We are seeing it in all its utter horror and foulness and malignity. There is no question but that God, in order to teach mankind the exceeding sinfulness of sin, sometimes withholds his restraining power, and allows the ungodly to have their fling. He gives them rope and the whole state of things appears in its true colours. Sin is ignored by the philosophers; the psychologists attempt to explain it away. But we are seeing it for what it is – this horrible foul perversion and lust. It is there in the heart of the educated as well as the illiterate, in every class and stratum of society.

That is one reason. But it is not the only reason; for there is no doubt but that God permits this kind of thing also partly as the punishment of sin. If you read Romans 1, you will find that this point comes out there also. In other words, God withdraws his restraining power sometimes in order that people may reap some of the consequences of their own sins, and thereby he punishes them. We are all one by nature in that we want the pleasure of sin without the consequences; we desire to be able to sin and not to suffer for it. But we cannot, for, 'There is no peace, saith my God, to the wicked.' God has so made mankind, and for that reason we shall suffer, and sometimes God allows the world to get into a state of godlessness as part of its punishment. I do not hesitate to assert that that is the only real explanation of the two world wars. It is, in part, God meting out punishment to mankind for all its defiance of him since the last century. God allows things to develop in order that mankind may reap the consequences of that which it has sown. If we 'sow the wind' we may well 'reap the whirlwind'. And we have experienced that in our own lifetime.

What is the next thing? I believe that God allows the evil and the evil-doers to have their fling; he allows them rope, licence, as it were, in order to make their overthrow more complete and sure. Biblical history is really an exposition of this principle. God seems to be asleep and the enemy rises. He blasphemes the name of God. Think of it in the case of Assyria. They set themselves against the God of Israel, and God allowed it all to happen. They inflated themselves almost to the heavens and said, 'Nothing can stop us.' Then God suddenly pricked the bubble and the whole empire collapsed, and the final discomfiture was very great. It is when the great big bully has made his final boast that he is brought down. If God had brought him down at the beginning it would not have seemed so wonderful. So God allows evil and evil powers to do astounding things to the world, so much so that even the godly begin to ask, Can God ever stop this? Then, when the end has almost come, God arises and down they go. The discomfiture of the enemy is greater then and more complete.

Then, again, God allows it in order to display his own greatness and glory in the defeat of such a great and mighty enemy. God arises and he demolishes him, and all who see it fear this almighty, glorious God. All this is well illustrated at the end of Acts 12. A king called Herod seated upon a throne made a great oration to certain people, and after he had delivered his oration the people cried out saying, 'It is the voice of a god, and not of a man.' Then God, we are told, sent an angel and smote this man 'because he gave not God the glory'. 'And he was eaten of worms, and gave up the ghost. But the word of God grew and multiplied.' You see the contrast. The pomp and the greatness were demolished; but the word of the God whom the foolish king was trying to destroy grew and multiplied, and so God's glory was manifested.

The last explanation I would put forward is this: There is no doubt at all but that God sometimes permits the ungodly to flourish for the sake of disciplining his own people. I am sorry to have to say that, but I must. We need to be disciplined. How often did God raise up enemies against the Children of Israel in order to discipline them. They, his own people, had become slack and were forgetting God. He pleaded with them, he sent them prophets but they paid no attention. So he raised up Assyria, he raised up the Chaldeans to chastise, to correct his own people. And I do not hesitate to assert that many of the things we have had to endure in this century have been, partly, at least, because we, God's people, have needed to be disciplined. It was, alas, the church herself that was largely responsible for undermining the faith of the people in the Word of God, and it is not surprising that things are now as they are. Maybe we shall have to endure much more in order that we ourselves may be humbled and brought low and brought to realize that we are God's people and that we must obey him and rely upon him and him alone.

There, it seems to me, are some of the answers given in the Scriptures as to why it is that God seems at times to be asleep.

But that does not exhaust what the Psalmist learned in the sanctuary about God's ways. He has been put right about the character of God, and sees that the explanation is that God only seems to be asleep. Then he ends with what happens when God does awake. 'How are they brought into desolation, as in a moment! they are utterly consumed with terrors. As a dream when one awaketh; so, O Lord, when thou awakest, thou shalt despise their image.' What is he saying? The first thing is that God does awake. 'When thou awakest.' It is going to happen. God is not permanently

137

asleep. When it does come . . . There is a limit to what God allows the ungodly. He certainly allows them to do a lot, but there is an end to the latitude and the apparent licence that he gives to his enemies. 'My spirit shall not always strive with man.' How long is this to go on? A key to the answer, given by God early in history, is that the godly must wait, 'for the iniquity of the Amorites is not yet full'. There is a limit. God does awake. God will awake.

What happens when he does awake? This man tells us very clearly what is going to happen then to these successful, ungodly people. He says, 'As a dream when one awaketh; so, O Lord, when thou awakest, thou shalt despise their image.' What a picture! That ungodly person, who seemed so great and marvellous, vanishes like a dream when God arises. It is as if he had been but a phantom, an image, an appearance, and had never been a reality. The ungodly who seemed so powerful, so self-sufficient and almost indestructible, when God arises are gone like a flash. The Bible is full of this. Read Isaiah 40 and you will see there that God says that to him the nations are but 'a drop of a bucket' and as 'the small dust of the balance'. These great nations with their atomic bombs and their hydrogen bombs, these mighty nations! They are but a drop in a bucket, or the small dust of the balance. And not only that. Listen to the sarcasm and the derision. All the nations of the earth 'are as grasshoppers', even Great Britain, the USA and the USSR! There have been other great empires and nations and commonwealths before; but they have all gone because they were not submissive to God. All the nations of the earth are but as grasshoppers – when God awakes.

Let me give you one other example; it is one of the most notable in history. You have read of Alexander the Great, so-called, one of the most skilful generals of all time, a great monarch and a mighty warrior. He conquered almost the entire known world. Do you know what the Scriptures call him? Read your Bible right through and you will never find the name of Alexander the Great. It is not mentioned. But Alexander the Great does come into the Scriptures, and you will find the way in which God refers to him in Daniel 8. As Walter Luthi has pointed out, he who to the world is Alex-

ander the Great, is to God 'a he-goat'! When God arises –
Alexander the Great becomes a he-goat! When God arises
that is what happens to nations, to empires, to individuals,
to all. 'When thou awakest': and he has awoken. Read the
history recorded in the Bible and you will find that God does
arise, and when that happens his enemies are scattered and
brought to nothing.

The final message, however, that comes to us out of all
this is that these great events of history which have already
happened are but a pale adumbration, and at the same time
a mighty warning, of that which is to happen. The world is
godless; it is Christless; it ridicules the grace of God and the
Saviour of the world and especially the holy blood of his
cross. The world is arrogant and vaunts its sin. But the apostle
Paul, who had been greatly persecuted, writing his second
letter to the Thessalonians tells us what is going to happen:
'So that we ourselves glory in you in the churches of God
for your patience and faith in all your persecutions and tribulations that ye endure: which is a manifest token of the
righteous judgment of God, that ye may be counted worthy
of the kingdom of God, for which ye also suffer: seeing it is
a righteous thing with God to recompense tribulation to them
that trouble you; and to you who are troubled rest with us,
when the Lord Jesus shall be revealed from heaven with his
mighty angels, in flaming fire taking vengeance on them that
know not God, and that obey not the gospel of our Lord
Jesus Christ: who shall be punished with everlasting destruction from the presence of the Lord, and from the glory of
his power; when he shall come to be glorified in his saints,
and to be admired in all them that believe . . . in that day.'

This is as certain as the fact that we are alive at this moment.
The Lord will come riding upon the clouds of heaven and all
his enemies will be scattered and routed. Satan and hell and
all opposed to God will be cast into the lake of fire and go
to 'everlasting destruction from the presence of the Lord'.
That is the end of the ungodly. That is the power and the
glory of the God whom we love and whom we adore and
serve. If you do not understand what is happening, put it
into that context. God is God. God is holy and just. What
he has promised he will certainly perform. He permits these

139

things for his own ends. A day is coming when he will arise and scatter his enemies, and the kingdom of Jesus Christ will stretch 'from shore to shore' and 'at the name of Jesus every knee should bow, of things in heaven, and things in earth, and things under the earth; And that every tongue should confess that Jesus Christ is Lord, to the glory of God the Father'.

Thank God that his promises are ever sure. God grant that we all may see and know and understand God's ways and be rid, once and for ever, of all sinful doubt and unworthy questioning.

Chapter Six

SELF-EXAMINATION

Thus my heart was grieved,
and I was pricked in my reins.
So foolish was I, and ignorant:
I was as a beast before thee.

Here we come to yet a further stage in this man's account of
the crisis through which he had passed in his soul and in his
godly walk. We have seen him put right in his thinking about
the ungodly, and in his thinking about God.

Now we come to a consideration of how he was put right
in the third respect, in his thinking about himself. This he
describes in a striking and severe manner in the two verses
we are now considering. Notice first the striking contrast
they present to what he has previously said about himself in
verses 13 and 14. There he said, 'Verily I have cleansed my
heart in vain, and washed my hands in innocency: For all the
day long have I been plagued, and chastened every morning.'
He is very sorry for himself. There is nothing wrong with
his life. He is a very good man. But he is being very hard
pressed, he is being dealt with very unfairly, and even God
seems to be unfair to him. That is how he thought about
himself while he was outside the sanctuary. But inside the
sanctuary all this is changed, 'Thus my heart was grieved,
and I was pricked in my reins. So foolish was I, and ignorant:
I was as a beast before thee.' What a transfiguration! What
an entirely different view of himself! And it is all the result
of his thinking being put right, and made truly spiritual.

Now this is a most important matter, and a most important

point in the whole movement of the teaching of this Psalm. Let us be quite frank and honest and admit that we are very prone to stop short of this point. We are all quite happy to read about the ungodly – and I do not know anybody who has been upset about a sermon which shows how the ungodly have been set in slippery places. Then there is that great and exalted doctrine about God – 'the Lord reigneth'. We all like to hear about that. We accept the teaching about the judgment of the ungodly, and we like to read about the glory and the majesty of God, because that makes us feel that everything is going to be right for us. The danger for us is to stop at that point and to go no farther. This man, however, goes on, and as he does so he not only reveals his honesty and his sincerity, and the truthfulness that was so essentially a part of his make-up, but also – and this is the thing I want to emphasize – he displays an understanding of the nature of the spiritual life.

In these two verses we have this man's account of his repentance. We learn what he said to himself about himself and, in particular, about his recent conduct. It is, indeed, a classic example of honest self-examination. I invite you to consider it with me because of its important bearing on Christian discipline. This repentance, this state in which someone pauses and looks at himself and talks to himself about himself, is one of the most essential and vital aspects of what is commonly called the discipline of the Christian life. I do not apologize for emphasizing this again, because it is a matter which is being seriously neglected at the present time. How often do we hear about the discipline of the Christian life these days? How often do we talk about it? How often is it really to be found at the heart of our evangelical living? There was a time in the Christian church when this was at the very centre, and it is, I profoundly believe, because of our neglect of this discipline that the church is in her present position. Indeed, I see no hope whatsoever of any true revival and reawakening until we return to it.

As we approach this great subject let me start by saying that there seem to me to be two main dangers in connection with it, and of course, as is usually the case, they are at opposite extremes. We are creatures given to extremes, taking up our position either at one end or the other. The difficulty is to walk in the right position, avoiding all violent reactions; for the true position in the Christian life is generally in the middle, between the two extremes. One danger that used to be fairly common was the danger of morbidity and introspection. I would say that it is not the commonest difficulty with Christian people at the present time, though some are certainly still subject to it. I believe it is true to say that in some parts of Great Britain, as, for instance, in the Highlands of Scotland, you will still find the thing to which I am referring. At one time it was certainly very common there and elsewhere among Celtic people. I myself was brought up in a religious atmosphere given to this tendency, where people spent much, if not all, of their lives in analysing and condemning themselves, conscious only of their unworthiness and their lack of fitness. As a result of this attitude people become introspective, and turn inwards on themselves. They are always feeling their own spiritual pulse and taking their own spiritual temperature, and they become almost submerged in this process of self-condemnation.

Let me tell you the story of one of the most pathetic scenes I have ever witnessed. I was at the death-bed of one of the saintliest and most godly men I have ever been privileged to meet. In the room were his two daughters – both of them well on into middle age. The old man, the father, knew he was dying, and the one thing he was unhappy about was the fact that neither of his daughters was a church member, or had ever taken Communion. It was a truly astounding fact, because two women more godly or more active in connection with the life of the church which they attended would be hard to find. But they were not church members. Why had they never taken Communion? The answer was that they felt unworthy of it; they felt they were not fit to come to the Table, so conscious were they of their failures and of their sins and shortcomings. Here were two most excellent Christian women, but because of this introspection, because they turned in upon themselves, they felt they had no right to partake in the inner life of the church.

Now that kind of thing was once very common. People would stand up in church meetings just to say that they were terrible sinners, and to stress how much they had failed. They

143

hoped they would arrive in heaven, but they could not see how such worthless creatures could ever get there. You may be familiar with such an attitude from your reading. It was certainly a tendency in the lives of the saintly John Fletcher and Henry Martyn. They were not extreme cases; but they obviously had that tendency, and it was a feature of the piety of that age.

But that is by no means the danger today, especially not, if I may say so, here in London and in the circles in which most of us move. Indeed, the danger among us is quite different; it is the danger against which the prophet Jeremiah warns us when he speaks of those who 'have healed also the hurt of the daughter of my people slightly, saying, Peace, peace; when there is no peace'. It is the opposite extreme from the other tendency. It is the absence of a true godly sorrow for sin, together with the tendency to spare ourselves and to regard ourselves and our sins, our shortcomings and our failures, very lightly.

Let me put it still more drastically. I believe there is a very real danger among some, and among evangelical people in particular, of misusing the doctrine of salvation, misusing the great doctrines of justification by faith only and of the assurance of salvation, with a consequent failure to realize what sin really is in God's sight and what it really means in a child of God. The idea seems to have gained currency, I know not why, that repentance should play no part at all in the life of the Christian. There are people who seem to think it is wrong to speak of repentance. They say that the moment you see that you have sinned and then have put your sin 'under the blood' you are all right. To stop and think about it and to condemn yourself means that you lack faith. The moment you 'look to Jesus' all is well. We heal ourselves so easily; indeed, I do not hesitate to say that the trouble with most of us is that in a sense we are far too 'healthy' spiritually. I mean by that, that we are much too glib, and much too superficial. We do not take trouble in these matters; we, unlike the Psalmist in these two verses, are on much too good terms with ourselves. We are so unlike the people depicted in the Scriptures.

I suggest that this is due to the fact that we fail to go on to take the step which the man in this Psalm now took. In the sanctuary he was not only put right about the ungodly, and about God, but also about himself, and you notice the way in which he deals with himself. We do not seem to do that in these days, and the result is that there is this false appearance of health, as if all were well with us. There is very little sackcloth and ashes; there is very little godly sorrow for sin; there is very little evidence of true repentance.

Let me show you that the need for repentance and the importance of it are taught in the Scriptures everywhere. The classic example of this teaching is, of course, to be found in the parable of the Prodigal Son. There we have the story of someone who sinned, who in his folly left home and then found that things went wrong with him. What happened? When he came to himself, what did he do? He condemned himself, he spoke to himself about himself. He dealt with himself very severely. And it was only after doing that that he arose and went back to his father. Or take that wonderful statement in 2 Corinthians 7:9–11. These Christians in Corinth had committed a sin and Paul had written to them about it and had sent Titus to preach to them about it. Their subsequent action provides us with a definition of what is really meant by a true spirit of repentance. What pleased the great apostle about them was the way in which they dealt with themselves. You notice that he goes into it in detail. He says, 'For behold this selfsame thing, that ye sorrowed after a godly sort, what carefulness it wrought in you, yea, what clearing of yourselves, yea, what indignation, yea, what fear, yea, what vehement desire, yea, what zeal, yea, what revenge! In all things ye have approved yourselves to be clear in this matter.' These Corinthian people had dealt severely with themselves and had condemned themselves; they had 'sorrowed after a godly sort', and because of that Paul tells them that they are again in the place of blessing.

Another wonderful example of the same thing comes in the book of Job. You remember how Job throughout the main part of that book is justifying himself, defending himself and sometimes feeling sorry for himself. But when he came truly into the presence of God, when he was in the place where he met with God, this is what he said, 'Wherefore I abhor myself, and repent in dust and ashes' (42:6). There was no more godly man than Job, the most upright, the most religious man in the world. But now, because of his adversity, he no longer remembers the good things that had happened to him nor all the blessings he had enjoyed. Job had been tempted to think of God in the same way as this man in Psalm 73, and he had said things he should not have said. But when he sees God he puts his hand on his mouth and says, 'I abhor myself, and repent in dust and ashes.' I wonder whether we know that experience. Do we know what it is to abhor ourselves? Do we know what it is to repent in dust and ashes? The popular doctrine of our times does not seem to like that, because it teaches that we have passed out of Romans 7. We must not talk about sorrow for sin because that would mean that we are still in the very early stages of the Christian life. So we pass over Romans 7 and turn to Romans 8. But have we ever been in Romans 7? Have we ever really said from the heart, 'O wretched man that I am! who shall deliver me from the body of this death?' Have we ever really abhorred ourselves and repented in dust and ashes? This is a very vital part of the discipline of the Christian life. Read the lives of the saints throughout the centuries and you will find that they did it very frequently. Go back to Henry Martyn, for example; go back to any of those mighty people of God, and you will find that they frequently abhorred themselves. They hated their lives in this world; they hated themselves in that sense. And it was because of this that they were so mightily blessed of God.

Nothing is more important, therefore, than for us to follow the Psalmist and see exactly what he did. We must learn to turn upon ourselves and to deal with ourselves faithfully. It is a vital matter in the Christian life. What are the steps? I have tried to divide them in the following way.

First and foremost we must really confess what we have done. Now we do not like doing that. We are aware of what we have done, and our tendency is to say, 'I turn to Christ, and at once I am forgiven and all is well.' That is an error. We must confess what we have done. This man had spent a lot of time in commiserating with himself, in looking at other people and envying them. He had spent a lot of time with unworthy thoughts about God and his ways. But after his recovery in the sanctuary he says to himself, 'I must spend an equal amount of time in looking at myself and looking at what I have done.' We must not spare ourselves. We must really confess what we have done, which means that we must deliberately hold these things before ourselves. We must not shield ourselves in any way; we must not attempt to slide over our sin; we must not merely take a casual glance at it. We must hold the facts before ourselves deliberately and say, 'This is what I did; this is what I thought and what I said.'

But not only that. I must analyse this thing and I must work it out in all its details and consider all that it involves and implies. This is something that by means of self-discipline we have to do quite relentlessly and resolutely. This man undoubtedly did so. That is why he ends by saying, 'I was as a beast.' He confessed, 'I actually thought that about thee, O God, and I was on the point of saying it – that is what I really did.' He put it before himself and he held it there until he was crushed to the ground and felt he was 'as a beast'. We shall never really abhor ourselves unless we do that. We have to hold our sin before us until we really see it for what it is.

Let me emphasize that we have to particularize and to descend to details. I know this is very painful. We have to particularize and that means that it is not enough just to come to God and say, 'God, I am a sinner.' We must bring it down to details, we must confess to ourselves and to God in detail what we have done. Now it is easier to say, 'I am sinful,' than it is to say, 'I have said something I should not have said, or thought something I should not have thought,' or 'I have harboured an unclean thought.' But the essence of this matter is to get right down to details, to particularize, to put it all down on paper, to put every detail down before yourself, to analyse yourself and to face the horrible character of sin in detail. That is what the masters in the spiritual life have always done. Read their manuals, read the journals of the most saintly people who have adorned the life of the church, and you will find that they have always done that. I have reminded you of John Fletcher. He not only asked twelve questions of himself before he went to sleep each night but he got his congregation to do the same. He did not content himself with a cursory general examination; he explained himself in detail, with such questions as: Do I lose my temper? Have I lost my temper? Have I made life more difficult for somebody else? Did I listen to that insinuation that the devil put into my mind, that unclean idea? Did I cling to it or immediately reject it? You go through the day and you put it all before yourself and face it. That is true self-examination.

Then we must view it all in the sight of God – 'before thee'. We must take all these things and ourselves into the presence of God, and before we speak to God we must condemn ourselves. You notice Paul's word in 2 Corinthians 7:11, 'Yea, what indignation.' They were indignant with themselves. Our trouble is that we are not indignant with ourselves, and we should be, because we are all guilty of the sins I have been enumerating. These are horrid things in the sight of God, and we are not indignant. We are on too good terms with ourselves; that is why our witness is so ineffective. We must learn to humble ourselves, we must learn to humiliate ourselves, we must learn to strike ourselves. Paul tells us in 1 Corinthians 9:27, 'I keep under my body.' Metaphorically he pummels it, he beats it until it is black and blue – that is the derivation of this word he uses, the word translated 'keep under'. And we must do the same. It is an essential part of the discipline. Undoubtedly this man did it, because he ends by saying, 'So foolish was I, and ignorant: I was as a beast before thee.' It is only a man who has gone through the process of self-examination thoroughly who comes to that view. If we therefore are to come to that we must persist in the way I have indicated and truly search ourselves in order that we may see ourselves for what we really are.

The next point for our consideration is this. What is it we discover when we have done all that? There can be no doubt at all as to the answer given in this Psalm. What this man found when he examined himself and really began to think correctly about himself was that the great cause, if not, indeed, the only cause of all his troubles was 'self'. That is always the trouble. Self is our last and our most constant enemy; and it is the most prolific cause of all our unhappiness. As a result of the fall of Adam we are self-centred. We are sensitive about ourselves. We are always selfish, always protecting ourselves, always ready to imagine offences, always ready to say that we have been wronged and dealt with unfairly. Am I not speaking from experience? May God have mercy upon us. It is the truth about us all. Self, this enemy that even tries to make us proud of our own humility. The Psalmist found that that really was the cause of all his troubles. He had gone wrong in thinking about the ungodly, he had gone wrong in thinking about God. But the ultimate cause of all his troubles was that he had gone wrong in thinking about himself. It was because he was always revolving around himself that everything else seemed to be so terribly wrong and grossly unfair.

I want to introduce you to the psychology taught in this verse – true biblical psychology. I wonder whether you noticed it. When self takes control of us something inevitably happens. Our hearts begin to control our heads. Listen to this man. He has recovered himself in God's house; he has been put right about the ungodly and about God. Now he comes to himself and says, 'My heart was grieved, and I was pricked in my reins' – again a part of the sensibility – 'So foolish was I, and ignorant: I was as a beast before thee.' You notice the order. He puts the heart before the head. He points out that it was his heart that was grieved before his brain began to function wrongly – heart first and then head.

Now this is one of the profoundest bits of psychology we can ever grasp. The real trouble is that the self, when it asserts itself, causes this reversal of the true order and of the right sense of proportion. All our troubles are ultimately due to the fact that we are governed by our feelings and our hearts and sensibilities instead of by clear thinking and the honest facing of things before God. The heart is a very powerful faculty within us. When the heart gets into control it bludgeons a person. It makes us stupid; it takes hold of us so that we become unreasonable and unable to think clearly. That is what happened to this man. He had thought it was a pure question of fact – there are the ungodly, look at them and look at me! He thought that he was very rational. But he discovered in the sanctuary that he was not rational at all but that his thinking had been governed by his feelings.

149

Is not this the trouble with all of us? The apostle Paul puts the whole matter in a great word in Philippians 4:6, 7. Observe the order of the words. 'Be careful for nothing [be over-anxious for nothing]; but in every thing by prayer and supplication with thanksgiving let your requests be made known unto God.' What will happen? The next verse tells us. 'And the peace of God, which passeth all understanding, shall keep your minds and hearts'? Not at all! 'The peace of God, which passeth all understanding, shall keep your hearts and minds through Christ Jesus.' Hearts first, then minds in this matter, because here the trouble is mainly in the realm of feelings.

That is profound psychology. The apostle Paul was a master physician in treating diseases of the soul. He knew that it was quite pointless to deal with the mind until the heart was put right, so he puts the heart first. The trouble with anyone in this condition who feels that he is having a hard time and that things are not going right is that he begins to question God; whereas the root of the matter is that his heart is disturbed and he is being governed and controlled by it. His feelings have taken possession of him and have blinded him to everything else.

All the troubles and quarrels and disputes in life are ultimately due to this. All family quarrels, all disputes between husbands and wives, all quarrels between relatives, all quarrels between classes and groups, all quarrels between nation and nation can be put down to the fact that self is being controlled by feelings. If we stopped to think we should see how wrong it is, because what we are really saying is that we are absolutely perfect and everybody else is wrong. But patently that cannot be true because all are saying the same thing. We are all governed by this feeling about ourselves and we all tend to say, 'People are not fair to me, I am always being misunderstood, people are always doing things to me.' And the other people are saying exactly the same thing. The trouble is that we are being controlled by self, we are living on our feelings, and in a most extraordinary way we are being governed by them.

We all know this from experience. We take our stand and we say, 'I don't see why I should give in.' We hold on to it.

We even put an emphasis on it unconsciously: 'I? What have I done? Why should I be treated like this?' 'My heart was grieved, and I was pricked in my reins'; it is always the heart. The principle I would emphasize is that when self is in the ascendant it always plays on our feelings. Self cannot stand up to a real intellectual examination. If, as I say, we only sat down and thought about it we should realize what fools we are. For then we would say, 'I feel like this, but so does the other person. I say this, but he also says this. Obviously we both think we are right. We must both be to blame and I am as bad as he is.' 'He that is down,' says John Bunyan, 'needs fear no fall, He that is low, no pride.'

We must learn to keep a careful watch on our hearts. It is not surprising that the Scripture says, 'My son, give me thine heart.' It is not surprising that Jeremiah says, 'The heart is deceitful above all things, and desperately wicked.' How foolish we are in our psychology. We tend to say of people, 'Well, you know, he is not very intellectual; he does not understand very much, but he has a good heart.' That is quite wrong. However unintelligent we may be, our minds are much better than our hearts. Generally speaking, people are not wrong because they think, but because they do not think.

This poor man in Psalm 73 was being controlled by his heart, but he did not know it. He thought he was reasoning out facts. The heart is 'deceitful'; it is so clever and subtle. That is why we must watch it. 'This is the condemnation,' we read in John 3:19, 'that light is come into the world, and men loved darkness rather than light, because their deeds were evil.' It is the heart that is wrong, so we end with the advice of the wise man in Proverbs 4:23, 'Keep thy heart with all diligence; for out of it are the issues of life.' Watch your heart, watch yourself, watch your feelings. When your heart is sour everything will be sour and nothing will be right. It is the heart that governs everything and there is only one final treatment for this sour and bitter heart. It is to come to God as the Psalmist came, and to realize that God in his infinite love and grace, in his mercy and compassion sent his Son into the world to die upon the cross that we should come to abhor ourselves, that we might be forgiven and once more have a clean heart, that David's prayer might be answered, 'Create in me a clean heart, O God.' That prayer is answered in Christ. He can cleanse the heart and sanctify the soul:

> *'Tis thine to cleanse the heart,*
> *To sanctify the soul,*
> *To pour fresh life in every part,*
> *And new create the whole.*

Once a person gets to know himself and the blackness and deceitfulness of his own heart, he knows that he has to fly to Christ. And there he finds forgiveness and cleansing, a new life, a new nature, a new heart, a new name. Thank God for a gospel that can give us a new heart and renew a right spirit within us.

Chapter Seven

SPIRITUAL ALLERGY

Thus my heart was grieved,
and I was pricked in my reins.
So foolish was I, and ignorant:
I was as a beast before thee.

In these two verses, as we have seen, the Psalmist tells us how he came to see that he had been entirely wrong, not only in his thinking about the ungodly, and about God, but also in his thinking about himself. The first thing he discovered was that self after all is the real trouble, and it is because self tends to get into control that so many of our difficulties and problems and perplexities in this life arise. That is the key to everything. We emphasized that this man was very honest with himself; indeed, he was quite brutal. And as we proceed, that will become still more evident. He did not take a mere cursory glance at himself and then forget all about it and go on to something else. He just stood and looked at himself, he looked steadfastly into that mirror and faced himself down to the smallest detail. He flinched at nothing.

That is absolutely essential. There is no possible growth in the Christian life unless we are ruthlessly honest with ourselves. Of all aspects of the Christian life self-examination is, perhaps, the one most neglected today. This is partly because of erroneous teaching, but also because we do not like doing anything that is painful to ourselves. There is no question about the teaching. Nothing is so characteristic of the true saint as the way in which he examines himself, faces himself and deals ruthlessly with himself. The Psalmist did that, and he had to admit that self was really the source of his troubles.

Then we saw that he discovered this other very interesting thing, that, when self is in control, it generally happens that the heart takes control of the thinking. It is a very sad state of affairs when our minds are governed by our hearts. That was never meant to be the case. The mind, the understanding, is mankind's supreme gift; it is undoubtedly a part of the image of God in human beings. The power to reason and to understand and to think and to know why we do things, and whether or not we ought to be doing them, is one of the things that differentiates us from animals. So, when we find ourselves thinking emotionally, if I may use such a term, we are in a very bad condition. The Psalmist had got into that condition where the heart came before the head. The Bible is very concerned about this, and its teaching everywhere is that we should always guard the heart, because 'out of it are the issues of life'. That means that it must be under the control of truth. So we are urged to 'seek wisdom' and to 'get knowledge'. We must never give the impression that people become Christian by ceasing to think and by just responding to their hearts. A Christian is one who believes and accepts and surrenders himself to the truth. He see it, is moved by it and acts upon it. The term 'heart' in Scripture does not mean the emotions only, but includes the mind; and repentance means a change of mind.

Let us now go on to consider what this man discovered about himself in detail. He tells us in these two verses. The first thing he discovered when he really saw the position truly was that he had very largely been producing his own troubles and his own unhappiness. He found in the sanctuary of God that his trouble was not really the ungodly at all; it was himself. He found that he had, to use our phrase, 'worked himself up' into this condition. Now let me give you the evidence for that. Verse 21 in the Authorized Version reads, 'Thus my heart was grieved, and I was pricked in my reins.' This translation rather suggests that something had happened to his heart; something had happened to his 'reins', his kidneys, another seat of the feelings and emotions according to ancient psychology. But what this man actually said was something slightly different. These words which are used in verse 21 are reflexive. What he is saying is that he had done something to himself. He is saying, 'I have soured my heart.' And as regards the reins you can translate like this, 'I was preparing for myself a piercing pain.' He had been doing it himself. He had been stimulating his own heart, he had been exacerbating his own trouble, he had been souring his own feelings. He himself had really been producing his own troubles and giving rise to this piercing pain which he had been enduring until he went into the sanctuary of God.

This is clearly a very important and vital principle. The fact is, and must we not all confess it in the presence of God at this moment, that we tend to produce and to exacerbate our own troubles. We, of course, tend to say, as this man had been saying before he went to the sanctuary of God, that it is that thing outside us that produced all the trouble. But it is not that thing at all; it is ourselves. I remember reading once a phrase which I think puts this point quite well, 'It is not life that matters, but the courage that you bring to it.' Now I do not accept that philosophy of courage, but I am quoting the phrase because, though it is wrongly stated, there is an essential element of truth in it. 'It is not life that matters.' Well, what does matter? It is you and I and the way we face it, the way we react, our behaviour with respect to it. I can prove that quite simply. You may see two persons living exactly the same sort of life, facing precisely the same conditions. And yet they are very different. One is bitter and sour and grumbling and complaining; the other is calm and quiet, happy and composed. Where is the difference? It is not in the conditions; it is not in what is happening to them. It is something in *them;* the difference is in the two persons themselves.

Now this can be demonstrated abundantly. There is a couplet that puts it well:

> *Two men looked out from prison bars.*
> *The one saw mud, the other stars.*

One, you see, looked down; the other looked up. It is not life, it is not the circumstances, it is not the ungodly, it is not

155

these things, it is us. This man discovered all that, discovered that he had been creating and exaggerating and exacerbating his own troubles. He had been souring his own heart.

God knows we all tend to be guilty of the same thing. It is not the external cause itself that matters. The particular thing is there, of course, but it is very important that we should realize that it is the way in which we react to that thing that determines what is going to happen to us, not merely the thing in and of itself. We have a phrase which I think puts this very well. We say of a certain type of person, 'He is always making a mountain out of a molehill.' There was something there, of course; even a molehill is something. There must be something to work on. But the thing itself was very small; it really was just a molehill. This person, however, was making a mountain of it; he had worked it up into something tremendous. He therefore thought that he was confronted by a mountain of trouble, but really he was not. He had turned the molehill into a mountain. So it is that we, too, bother ourselves and agitate ourselves and get into this same condition.

We have another phrase which describes it. We say that we become 'worked up' about something. Now that is not quite accurate. It is not so much that we become worked up as that we work ourselves up. In other words, the reaction is too big for the stimulus. That is obviously the case because we are not properly balanced, we are not in a right condition, we are hyper-sensitive. Everybody today is talking about being 'allergic' to things; it is one of the current phrases. Now what does that mean? It means that you are hyper-sensitive. There are some people, for instance, who cannot be in the same room as a cat without having an attack of asthma. Others cannot be near a field of hay without having an attack of hay fever. You are familiar with all that. What is the matter? The authorities say it is the dust or the pollen in the air. But it is not simply the pollen, of course, because other people can walk in the same field and nothing happens to them. The pollen is there. But the point is that these people suffer from hay fever not because of the pollen but because they are hyper-sensitive, they are allergic. Now that illustrates the thing the Psalmist discovered. But he goes beyond that, and rightly so. He says that he worked up the sensitivity, indeed hyper-sensitivity. It can be done quite easily. You can make your heart hyper-sensitive. You can tend it and fondle it, and the more you do so the more your heart will like it, and the more sensitive and sorry it will be for itself. You can so work it up into this condition that the slightest thing will cause trouble at once. If you strike a match – just one match – in a barrel of gunpowder there will be a terrible explosion. It is not the match that counts primarily, it is the barrel of gunpowder.

That is the kind of thing this man discovered. He had been totally wrong in his thinking about the ungodly. He thought that they alone were the cause of his problem. But he discovered that it was not anything of the kind. He had worked up his heart into this foolish condition; he was hyper-sensitive. And so he was in such a state that when the slightest thing went wrong it would cause an explosion. I am sure we all realize the truth of what I am saying, but the question is, do you see yourself doing that very same thing? Every time you talk to yourself about yourself do you feel sorry for yourself? If so, you are doing what this man had been doing; you are increasing this morbidity and hyper-sensitivity, and you are preparing yourself for a painful experience. This is what is called masochism. You are familiar with that kind of perversion of which we are all more or less guilty. It is a strange thing about human nature, and one of the appalling consequences of the Fall, that we take this perverse delight, as it were, in hurting ourselves. It is a most peculiar thing, but we enjoy our own misery because, while we are enjoying it, we are also pitying ourselves at the same time. That is where the subtlety of it all comes in. While we are thoroughly miserable and unhappy there is a sense in which we hold on to it because it gives a kind of perverted enjoyment. We are still protecting and magnifying self.

This man discovered all that in the sanctuary of God. He had been grieving himself; he had produced his own misery and he had kept it up. He had exaggerated the whole thing instead of facing it honestly. He was not in all this great trouble; he was not really having a hard time. He was just looking at things in such a way as to give himself a hard time

157

– foolish man that he was! Are we not all like him at times – foolish creatures that we are?

Now the opposite to all this is that blessed condition which is described in Philippians 4:11–13. Paul puts it like this, 'For I have learned, in whatsoever state I am, therewith to be content. I know both how to be abased, and I know how to abound: every where and in all things I am instructed both to be full and to be hungry, both to abound and to suffer need. I can do all things through Christ which strengtheneth me.' In other words, he has arrived at a condition in which he is no longer hyper-sensitive. He is in a condition in which it does not matter very much what happens to him; it is not going to disturb him. 'I have learned, in whatsoever state I am, therewith to be content.' That is the position in which all of us who are Christians should be. The person who is not a Christian is not there, and cannot possibly be there. He is like a barrel of gunpowder; you never know when there is going to be an explosion. The slightest pin-prick causes great trouble; he is hyper-sensitive because of self. But the apostle Paul had remembered what our Lord puts first to his disciples, namely, 'If any man will come after me, let him deny himself.' Self must be put out first. Then let him 'take up his cross, and follow me'. Because self is dethroned and put into the background, the disciple is not hyper-sensitive, and these things do not cause troubles and alarms and explosions. He is balanced because self is put out and he is living for Christ.

Let us examine ourselves in the light of this. Let us think of all our grievances; think of all our hardships, all the slights and insults and all the rest of the things we think have been heaped upon us, and all the misunderstandings. Let us face them in the light of this teaching, and I think we shall see at a glance that it is rather a miserable and sorry business. It is all worked up. There is nothing there really; we have just been making a mountain out of a molehill. If we could but make a list of the things that have upset us, how ashamed we should be. How small, how petty we can be!

The next thing this man discovered was that he had become stupid. The Authorized Version translates verse 22, as, 'So foolish was I.' But that word really means 'stupid' and a much better word it is. He was like a beast, utterly irrational, behaving in a stupid, absurd manner. But this is always true of the condition that we are describing and analysing. What does it mean exactly? He says, 'So stupid was I, and ignorant.' 'I was' – he repeats the emphasis – 'I was as a beast before thee.' Again let us note his honesty, his truthful dealings with himself. He does not spare himself at all; he has seen the truth about himself and he states it – 'I was as a beast before thee.'

What does it mean? First and foremost it means that he was behaving instinctively. What is the difference between a beast and a person? I have already partly suggested the answer. Surely God's supreme gift to us is understanding and reason and the power to think. The animal may be highly intelligent; but it lacks that true quality and faculty of reason, however much it may sometimes appear to the contrary. It lacks the power to stand outside itself, to consider itself and its actions. It is we alone who can do that, and that is a part of the image of God in us. But the animal does not do that, the animal acts instinctively. I need not spend much time illustrating what I mean. But take the question of the migration of birds. A study of these matters makes it obvious that instinct rather than intelligence governs that marvellous phenomenon. In other words, animal behaviour is a matter of instinctive response to a given stimulus. Well, this man tells us that he had been behaving like that. In other words, he did not stop to think; he did not stop to ponder and reason about his problem. To be stupid means not to think logically, not to think clearly. You and I are meant to think logically, we are meant to think rationally, we are meant to think consecutively. But this man had not been thinking like that, he had been like the animal. The animal responds to the stimulus immediately and mechanically, without any interval for thought. The Psalmist had been doing that. And we all must see, when we begin to think about this, how prone we all are to do the same thing. It is very un-Christian, however.

One of the great differences between a Christian and a non-Christian should be that the Christian always puts in an interval between the stimulus and the response. The Christian should always put everything into another context. He should think about it; he should not jump to conclusions; he should

work the thing out. In other words, and surely this is very
vital and important, one of the hallmarks of the Christian
should be the capacity to think, to think logically, clearly and
spiritually. Now is not that the whole object of the New
Testament Epistles? What do they say? They reason with us.
These Epistles were given to Christian people like ourselves
who had their problems and perplexities, and what they all
say is just this, 'Don't just react to these things. Think about
them; put them into the context of the purposes of God;
relate them to the whole view of salvation and the Christian
life. And having done that you will find that you will think
about them in a different way.' The Christian is someone
who thinks in a different manner from the non-Christian. His
thinking is logical, clear, calm, controlled and balanced; and
above everything else it is spiritual. He thinks everything out
in terms of this great truth that he has here in the New
Testament. But the animal cannot do that. 'I was as a beast
before thee; I was stupid.' That kind of behaviour is not only
like an animal's, it is more or less like a child's also. A
child behaves like that because its reasoning faculty has not
sufficiently advanced and developed. It jumps to conclusions;
it reacts to stimuli like the animal. It has to be trained to
think and to reason, and not to be stupid.

Another way in which the Psalmist found that he had been
stupid was this. He had obviously held an idea of the godly
life which was quite false. He desired pleasure the whole time
and thought that his life was to be one long round of sunshine
and happiness. That was what had made him complain and
say, 'I have cleansed my heart in vain, and washed my hands
in innocency. For all the day long have I been plagued, and
chastened every morning.' Let me put this quite brutally and
plainly. Is not this true of all of us? We tend to take all the
gifts and the pleasures and the happiness and the joy without
saying much to God about it. But the moment anything goes
wrong we begin to grumble. We take our health and strength,
our food and clothing and our loved ones, all for granted.
But the moment anything goes wrong we start grumbling and
complaining and we say, 'Why should God do this to me?
Why should this happen to me?' How slow we are to thank,
how swift to grumble. But that is like the animal, is it not?

The animal likes to be petted and patted. He eats and enjoys his food. But the moment you correct him he does not like it. That is typical of the animal, and it is typical of the child outlook. The child will take all you give it. But if you with-hold something it wants, it resents it. That is being stupid. That is the failure to think. That is the childish, stupid, beast-like attitude. But how true it is; it was true of this man and it is true of us.

Let me put it like this. This man had been taking the blessings and the joys for granted. We all seem to assume that we have a right to these things and that we should have them always. Therefore the moment they are denied us we begin to question and to query. Now the Psalmist should have said to himself, 'I am a godly man, I believe in God. I am living a godly life and I know certain things about the character of God. These are beyond question. Now certain painful things are happening to me, and I see that the case of the ungodly is very different. But, of course, there must be some very good reason for this.' Then he should have begun to seek for reasons, and to look for an explanation. Had he done so he would undoubtedly have concluded that God had some purpose in all this. We have already considered some of those reasons. He would have to come to the conclusion that even though he might not understand it, God must have a reason, because God never does anything irrational. He would have said, 'I am certain of that, and, therefore, whatever the explanation is, it is not what I thought at first.' He would have thought it out.

But how slow we are to do that. We seem to think that, as Christian people, we should never have any trouble. Nothing should ever go wrong with us, and the sun should always be shining about us, while all who are not Christians, on the other hand, should know constant trouble and difficulty. But the Bible has never promised us that. It has rather promised 'that we must through much tribulation enter into the kingdom of God'. It says also, 'Unto you it is given in the behalf of Christ, not only to believe on him, but also to suffer for his sake' (Philippians 1:29). So the moment we begin to think, we see that the idea that came to us instinctively is utterly false to the teaching of the Bible.

Let me sum it all up like this. 'I was stupid; I was as a beast before thee' means that like beasts and animals, we always dislike discipline. We never see the need or the necessity for it. And whenever we are disciplined by God we tend to object and even to question and to query God's love and his goodness. Now that is something which this man describes perfectly when he says that that is to behave like a beast. No-one by nature likes to be disciplined. He wants to go on responding to his instincts; he does not like to be controlled. Animals always object to discipline, and in training them you have to be patient with them and sometimes you have to be severe, for this very reason.

Now this is characteristic of the immature Christian, the babe in Christ. Such a person resents discipline, and yet the answer to that is plain and unequivocal. The author of the Epistle to the Hebrews does not hesitate to use a striking and almost surprising phrase. He says, 'If you are not experiencing chastisement there is only one explanation for it and that is you are not children of God, you are bastards' (see Hebrews 12:8). If you are a child of God then you are certainly going to be disciplined, because God is preparing you for holiness. He is not an indulgent father who hands out sweets indiscriminately and does not care what happens to us. God is holy, and he is preparing us for himself and for glory; and because we are what we are, and because sin is in us, and because the world is what it is, we must needs be disciplined. So he sends us trials and tribulations in order to pull us up, and to conform us to 'the image of his Son'. But we do not like it, and like the animal we squeal because we dislike pain. But if we thought, if we were not stupid, we would even thank God for the pain. We would say with the writer of Psalm 119, 'It is good for me that I have been afflicted.' I sometimes think that there is no better test of the Christian position than just that, that we can even thank God for trials and troubles and for chastisement, because we see that they have been used of God to bring us nearer and closer to himself.

The next thing this man found about himself is that he was ignorant. To be ignorant is not the same thing as to be stupid, but stupidity usually leads to ignorance. This man was ignorant about the true position of the ungodly; he was ignorant about God; he was ignorant about himself, and about the very nature of the life he was living. He had forgotten about the whole purpose of godly living. And if you and I react as this man reacted to trials and troubles, in the last analysis there is only one thing to say about us, and that is that we are ignorant.

What are we ignorant of? We are ignorant of everything the Bible says about the godly life, and we are especially ignorant about the New Testament Epistles, all of which have been written to enlighten this particular ignorance. So if we always grumble about God's dealings with us and complain of his chastisements, we are simply making the confession either that we do not know our Scriptures at all, and that we have never understood the New Testament, or else that we are wilfully ignorant, that we refuse to think and to apply what we know. We see these books, but we refuse to listen to the arguments and we refuse to allow them to apply themselves to us. 'Ignorant.' This man says, 'I was behaving as an ignoramus; I was behaving as if I knew nothing about thy purposes; I was behaving as if I were a mere tyro in these matters, as if I had never read or heard the history of the past.' And it is perfectly true of us also. The moment we allow our heart and our feelings to get into control we become hyper-sensitive or allergic in this sense; and we behave just as if we knew nothing but were ignorant and as a beast in the presence of God.

That brings us to the final matter, which is the worst of all. Listen, 'Thus I exacerbated my own heart and I pricked myself in my reins and gave myself pain. So stupid was I and so ignorant, like an ignoramus; indeed I was as a beast *before thee*.' I think that that was the thing that broke this man's heart, and it is the thing that ought to break all our hearts. You see, in the sanctuary of God this man realized that he had been thinking all these horrible, unworthy, foolish, stupid things actually in the presence of God. 'Before thee.' That is why he thought of himself as a beast. Fancy thinking these things, and being on the point of saying them, in the presence of God! What he had forgotten was that God is 'a discerner of the thoughts and intents of the heart', and

'Neither is there any creature that is not manifest in his sight: but all things are naked and opened unto the eyes of him with whom we have to do' (Hebrews 4:12, 13). If only we realized that, we should never again behave as this man did and as we, to our shame, have often done.

You and I are always in the presence of God. When therefore you are sitting in your corner and feeling sorry for yourself because you have been hurt, and because this or that has happened to you, just remember that all this is happening in the presence of God. And when you ask, 'Is God fair to me, is it right that I should be suffering while other persons are so prosperous?' remember that you are asking that, and thinking that thought about God, in his very presence. 'Before thee.' This man had forgotten the greatness of God. If only you and I were always to remember the greatness of God there are some things we should never do again. When we realize we are but as a fly, or a grasshopper, or even less in the presence of the Almighty, and that he could remove us out of existence as if nothing had happened, we shall no longer stand up and flaunt ourselves in his presence and begin to question him. We must realize, in the words of a wise man of the Old Testament, that 'God is in heaven, and thou upon earth'.

But, especially, we must remember the love of God. God is love. This man realized that he was a very stupid, foolish man to question the love of God. He owed everything to the love and goodness and graciousness of God. So when we think these hard, unworthy thoughts of God, we must remember that we are thinking about the One who so loved us that he sent his Son into the world and even to the shame and agony of Calvary for us. Yet we think these thoughts of such a God even in his very holy presence. Just picture yourself sulking in the presence of God, sulking like a spoilt child. Look at the little child sulking; look at the animal. How ridiculous they look. Well, multiply that by infinity and think of yourself in the presence of this almighty, holy, loving God. No, there is nothing to be said for this condition. The Psalmist is right; he is not being unkind to himself, he is stating the simple truth – 'I was as a beast, ignorant, utterly foolish.'

What is the opposite of this? I can think of nothing better than the condition of the Prodigal Son after he came to himself. I have no doubt that up to a point that poor fellow thought he had been hardly dealt with. He left home for the far country. He was going to assert himself, but things went wrong and he thought he was being harshly dealt with. Then he came to himself and he went home and said, 'Father, I have sinned against heaven, and in thy sight, and I am no more worthy to be called thy son.' That is just another way of saying exactly the same thing. Nothing to recommend us, no excuses; we have just been unutterably stupid, like beasts. We have failed to think and to reason; we have failed to apply these Scriptures. It is this horrible self that has been in control, and we are so hyper-sensitive that nothing and no-one is right but ourselves. Let us face it; let us unmask it; let us analyse it and face ourselves with it. Let us look at it honestly until we are heartily ashamed of ourselves. Then let us go to that gracious loving God and acknowledge that we are as worms and less before him, that we have no claim upon him at all, and no right to his forgiveness. Let us tell him that we do not wish to be healed quickly, that we feel we do not deserve to be healed at all.

As we saw before, the trouble with many of us is that we heal ourselves too quickly. We feel we have a right to be forgiven. But the teaching of the Scripture, and the example of the lives of the saints, is that, like the Prodigal Son, they deserved nothing but damnation, that they had been like beasts in their stupidity, and that they had no claim at all on God. Indeed, they were filled with amazement that God could forgive them. Let us examine ourselves in the light of that. Do we rush back to God feeling we have a right to forgiveness? Or do we feel we have no right to ask for forgiveness? That is how this man felt, and I suggest that that is how the true Christian always feels at first. Paul, after years of preaching, looked back across the past and said he was the 'chief' of sinners. He was still amazed that God could ever have forgiven him. Though he was an apostle, he still, as it were, felt that he could receive something in an evangelistic service! He was still reacting as a sinner; he was still amazed at the wondrous cross and the love of God in Jesus Christ our Lord. 'So stupid was I, so foolish; I was as a beast before thee.'

Chapter Eight

'NEVERTHELESS'

Nevertheless I am continually with thee:
thou hast holden me by my right hand.
Thou shalt guide me with thy counsel,
and afterward receive me to glory.

The course of the Psalmist's history during the attack to which he had been subjected by the devil, is a most thrilling story. We see this man going from step to step and stage to stage, and anyone who has been through this kind of experience will know that these steps are inevitable. It is important, therefore, that we should observe every move in this account. There are few things more profitable than to watch the recovery of a soul. We see the man now on his way up again from the depths, on the way to recovery; and at the moment we are still watching him as he deals with himself.

He has humiliated himself to the very dust, he has put on his sackcloth and ashes. He admits that there is nothing to be said for someone who sulks and behaves as he had done in the presence of God – 'before thee'. But thank God he does not stop at that. He goes on with this great and blessed word 'nevertheless'. Now this is one of those words which in a sense epitomizes the whole biblical message. It is a word like the word 'but'; it is a word that so often introduces the gospel. It marks the difference between knowing the gospel and not knowing it. Someone who does not know the gospel could in a sense have gone as far as this man had gone, but he would have stopped there. The Christian never stops there. The Christian having gone down begins to turn back. 'But', 'nevertheless' – and there comes the gospel. It comes here in the case of this man. This word 'nevertheless' is therefore a most important one; indeed, these two verses we are now considering are vital.

A very good way of testing whether we are truly Christian or not is just to ask ourselves whether we can say this 'nevertheless'. Do we know this blessed 'but'? Do we go on, or do we stop where we were at the end of verse 22? Now the natural person stops there; the best natural person never goes beyond that, and there are many such people in the world today. There are good people who are not Christian – moral people, conscientious people – and you read now and again that one of them has committed suicide. They commit suicide because they cannot say this 'nevertheless'. They end at the point of self-examination and then say: I am a failure, I have gone wrong, I have not done my duty. They turn upon themselves. That is perfectly right as far as it goes. We should do that. But the essential point that is emphasized in these verses is that you do not stop there. If you stop there you may well be on the road to suicide. And there are many who do stop there, most noble people in a natural sense. They condemn themselves and say, 'There is no use for a person such as I am.' They judge themselves useless and worthless, and out they go. But the Christian does not do that, and it is just at this point that the whole difference between the Christian and the non-Christian comes in. The Christian must go all along that line to that point. But it is just when he is at the end that the door of hope opens, and he utters this blessed 'nevertheless'.

This is an astounding and glorious word. It is, incidentally, the word in this text that connects what is going to follow with what has gone before. It is the vital connecting link. But not only that; it is at the same time the turning-point. We have been watching the Psalmist going down and down and down, and we have felt that he could not go any farther. He has humbled himself to the dust; and then he begins to look upwards – 'nevertheless'. Immediately he is on the way up; he has started to move, and he will go right on until he is able to say triumphantly, 'God is always good to Israel.' But he did not arrive at that point by a single jump from the depths. He went through the process we are now considering, he went again through various stages. There are rungs on this ladder which reaches to the top and it is a wonderful thing to watch this man climbing from step to step. Have you ever known this 'nevertheless', when you have been miserable and could see no hope, when the devil was pressing you and telling you to shut the windows and pull down the blinds, and you have been enveloped in darkness and despair? Have you known that blessed moment when a shaft of light appears through a chink somewhere, introducing a new hope and changing your whole attitude and condition? This is the delivering word 'nevertheless'.

Here it is in this Psalm. It is very interesting to observe how it happened. The logic of these things is most fascinating. This is how it worked. He reached the point where he said, 'So foolish was I, and ignorant: I was as a beast before thee.' That suddenly made him see it. The moment he said 'before thee', he said also, 'Nevertheless I am continually with thee.' In other words, 'I am still in thy presence.' And everything changed. It was the delivering word. Having condemned himself because he had sulked like this, and had been so foolish in the presence of God, he now says, 'But I am in the presence of God still – Nevertheless I am continually with thee.'

Now this is an astounding thing, and the Psalmist could not get over it. What amazed him at this point was that he was still in the presence of God. Do you see it? God had not blotted him out though he had been so foolish in his presence. Why did God not dismiss him? Why did God not show him the door and say. 'That is the end of you; you are unworthy'? But he had not. He was still in the presence of God. That was the thing that came to this man with a thrill of surprise and astonishment. He did not receive the fate he so richly deserved. What is it all due to?

This leads us to what I regard as the doctrine of these two verses, the whole doctrine of the grace of God. It is a new realization of God's amazing grace. If this Psalm teaches us one thing more than anything else, it is that all that is best and most wonderful in life is entirely and solely the result of the grace of God. If we do not grasp that, we are really profiting nothing from our long consideration of the Psalm. The great message of this Psalm is that 'We are debtors to mercy alone', all the way, from the beginning to the very end. The whole of our life is entirely due to the grace and the mercy of God. This man discovered that, and he puts it in this way, 'Nevertheless I am continually with thee.' 'This', he says in effect, 'is the astonishing thing, that I am still with thee, that thou dost still permit me to come into thy presence.' The amazing grace of God. What if he had allowed us to remain in that other condition of self-condemnation and despair, of seeing nothing but the truth about ourselves without any relief whatsoever? But he does not do that.

Now let us see how the story of this man illustrates the various aspects of the doctrine of the grace of God. Certain divisions of this doctrine used to be recognized when people were interested in doctrine and not simply in biblical study. Biblical study is of very little value if it ends in and of itself and is mainly a matter of the meaning of words. The purpose of studying the Scriptures is to arrive at doctrine. Here we have a wonderful exposition of the doctrine of the grace of God. Let us follow the subdivisions which once were so familiar.

The first must, of necessity, be God's saving grace. The first thing the Psalmist realized was that God, in spite of all that was so true of him, had forgiven him. Because if God had not forgiven him, he would not still be in the presence of God. If God had dealt with this man as he deserved to be dealt with, he would have been thrown out. He would never have been allowed to come back into the presence of God again. But that is not the case; he is still in the presence of God. And that is absolute proof to him that God had forgiven him.

The Psalms are full of this. You remember the statement in Psalm 103, 'He hath not dealt with us after our sins; nor rewarded us according to our iniquities.' What if he did! There is another Psalm which puts it like this, 'If thou, Lord, shouldest mark iniquities, O Lord, who shall stand?' (130:3). We are in the presence of God, and we are there for one reason only, namely, that with God there is mercy that he may be feared. We are in the presence of God because God's name is Love; we are here because 'God so loved the world [in its sin and arrogance and rebellion and shame], that he gave his only begotten Son, that whosoever believeth in him should not perish, but have everlasting life.' There would be no beginning of the Christian life were it not for this saving grace. It is in spite of us that God forgives us. We are Christian not because we are good people; we are Christian because, though we were bad people, God had mercy upon us and sent his Son to die for us. We are saved entirely by the grace of God; there is no human contribution whatsoever, and if you think there is, you are denying the central biblical doctrine. If you feel at this moment that there is anything in you to recommend you to God, you do not believe the gospel of this Psalmist or the gospel of the New Testament. We are 'debtors to mercy alone'. Look at this man; consider what he had been doing; consider what he had been about to say; consider his whole attitude in the presence of God. How could God forgive that? Why did he forgive? Was there anything to merit it? There was nothing at all.

There is only one way to approach God; it is to come to him and say with the Prodigal Son, 'I have sinned against heaven, and in thy sight, and am no more worthy to be called thy son.' I want to make this very plain and clear. If you feel you have any right to forgiveness you are not, as I understand it, a Christian. Grace means goodness and kindness to undeserving sinners. God was moved by nothing but his own love, his own compassion, his own mercy and his own grace. If you do not see that, there is only one explanation. It is that you have never seen your sin, you have not been through what this man describes in the previous phrase. If you had seen yourself as a beast, as a stupid fool, as an ignoramus, if you had really seen yourself like that in the sight of this holy God, there would be no need to argue about it.

Let me give you another definition of a Christian. He is someone who realizes that, though he cannot forgive himself, God has forgiven him; he is amazed at the fact that he is forgiven. He does not take it for granted. He does not come demanding it as a right. He has never done that. Rather he says:

> *Just as I am, without one plea*
> *But that thy blood was shed for me,*
> *And that thou bidd'st me come to thee,*
> *O lamb of God, I come.*

Or:

> *Nothing in my hand I bring,*
> *Simply to thy cross I cling;*
> *Naked, come to thee for dress;*
> *Helpless, look to thee for grace;*
> *Foul, I to the fountain fly;*
> *Wash me, Saviour, or I die.*

That is what this man is saying, 'Nevertheless I am still with thee.' In spite of what I have been and what I have done, I am still with thee, because of thy love, thy compassion, thy saving grace. It was in spite of the fact that the world is as it is that God sent his Son into it. How often does God say that in the Old Testament. How often does he remind the Children of Israel that he saved them from Egypt not because they were what they were. It was for his holy name's sake he did it; it was because of his love and compassion for his own people. And the New Testament places its great emphasis always on this same saving grace of God. 'While we were yet sinners', 'when we were yet without strength, in due time.' God has done it all, and he must have all the credit and all the glory. 'Nevertheless' – in spite of myself, in spite of what is true of me – 'I am still with thee.'

But let us follow the Psalmist. Having started with this first realization that, after all, God is dealing with him, he then begins to look back a little. 'Nevertheless I am continually with thee: thou hast holden me by my right hand.' What does he mean? We can look at it in two ways.

First of all, we look at God's restraining grace. 'Thou hast holden me by my right hand.' This is as if he were saying, 'When I was going down you were there. You pulled me back; you saved me.' The Fathers used to make a great deal of this restraining grace of God. We seem to have forgotten it. How often have you heard it mentioned, and why do we not use these great terms? We have become unbiblical, we have forgotten our doctrines. But what a glorious doctrine this is. What does it mean? The Psalmist meant that it was God who had held and restrained him from that terrible fall. This was his position – 'As for me, my feet were almost gone; my steps had well-nigh slipped.' Why did he not slip? He now begins to understand. He had not seen it until this point. What saved him was that God held him back by his right hand. It was God who steadied him at the moment just before his final fall. God took a further grip of him; and just when he was on the point of going, he held him.

The Psalmist did not see it like that at the beginning. He simply saw that he was on the point of saying things that should never be said because it would be an offence to God's people. But why had he suddenly seen this? What made him think like that? Where had that thought come from, 'If I say, I will speak thus; behold, I should offend against the generation of thy children'? The answer is that it came from God. God held him by the right hand and restrained him. God put the thought into his mind and the thought held him back. He now sees that, and so, in a sense, it becomes the great theme of this Psalm.

Psalm 37:24 expresses the same thought. The Psalmist there is describing the righteous person and he says, 'Though he fall, he shall not be utterly cast down: for the Lord upholdeth him with his hand.' It is the same thought. It is important that this truth be put plainly. The doctrine, you observe, does not say that the Christian never falls. Alas, he does; but he is never 'utterly cast down'. This doctrine concerns the backslider. Are we clear about it? A backslider is obviously someone who falls; but it is equally right to say that he is someone who is never utterly cast down. Some people do not understand this doctrine of the backslider. They say that if someone who appears to be Christian falls into sin then he has never been a Christian. They are quite wrong. Surprising things can happen to a Christian, and a Christian can do surprising things. But the doctrine concerning the backslider teaches that, though he may fall, he is not utterly cast down.

In other words, he always comes back; he does not remain in sin. He is someone who has what is called 'a temporary fall'. There are people who appear to be Christian, but who have never done more than give merely an intellectual assent to the truth. They have never been born again, and they ultimately renounce the truth. These are not backsliders. It is only of the true Christian that the term 'backslider' can be used.

Let me put this plainly by giving you an illustration. I remember a man whom I and others were quite certain was a Christian. But a time came when we had to watch that man doing terrible things. He had been delivered from a life of drunkenness and immorality. He was converted and became a fine Christian. He grew spiritually in an astounding manner. But that man subsequently did some terrible things. He again became guilty of adultery. Worse than that he robbed his own wife and altogether behaved in a most despicable manner. Many people began to say that that man had never been a Christian. But I said in spite of all, 'This man is still a Christian; this is backsliding. He is not going to end his life like that.' He went from bad to worse, and people said, 'Now will you admit that this man is not a Christian?' I said, 'This man is a Christian; he is living in hell at the moment, but he will come back.' And, thank God, he did come back; and he is still standing firm and rejoicing in his faith once more. He fell, but he was not utterly cast down.

This is almost a terrible doctrine, but it is true. The Bible does not say that when someone is born again he can never sin again. We know that is not true. It does not teach perfectionism. The Christian does sin; the Christian may sin, terribly, horribly. Read 1 Corinthians 5. The man there was guilty of a foul sin, but he came back. He was so bad that the apostle could do nothing but deliver him over to Satan. But that man was restored and he came back. Thank God for it. This is God's restraining grace. He seems to allow us sometimes to go very very far away, but if you are a child of God you will never get right away. It is impossible.

But what of Hebrews 6? The answer is that the people described there were never born again. They were a people who had come under the temporary influence of the Holy

Spirit. There is never a suggestion that they had ever received new life. I am speaking of the regenerate person, when I say that though he may go far away, he will never go right away. As he looks back across his life he says, 'O Love, that wilt not let me go.' God will never let you go finally. This man had well-nigh slipped, but he says, 'Thou hast holden me by my right hand.' He was not allowed utterly to fall.

But let us go on another step. There is another part of this doctrine concerning grace taught in this verse, and that is the doctrine of God's 'restoring grace'. It is in the same verse. 'Thou didst hold me by my right hand.' This is again a very wonderful part of the doctrine. As he looks back, the man is beginning to understand it all. He had come to see that God was holding his right hand, and that at the vital point he had pulled him back. But the Lord did not stop there. What was it that had brought the man right back? He was so miserable, so envious of the foolish. What was it that brought him back and enabled him to understand? Some may feel that that is an unnecessary question, because we have seen that it was entirely the result of his going to the sanctuary of God. He tells us that himself. 'When I thought to know this, it was too painful for me; until I went into the sanctuary of God; then understood I their end.' What restored the man was his decision to go to the sanctuary of God.

But that alone is a superficial answer. The question we must ask is this: What was it that made him go to the sanctuary of God? There he was, nursing his grievance and saying, 'It is unfair; God is not just. I have washed my hands and cleansed my heart, and yet I am always in trouble, while the ungodly are thoroughly happy.' The gospel did not seem to be true. Then he suddenly felt that he had to go to the sanctuary of God. But what took him there? There is only one answer to that; God's restoring grace. I suggest that he went there because God put it into his mind. As we say so glibly, it was something that 'occurred' to him. But why did it occur to him? The answer is, God put it into his mind.

Let me go back again to the Christian man who fell and became guilty of adultery and deceived and robbed his own wife. Here is the rest of his story. He left his home and came to London and was living in adultery. His money came to an end. He was wretched and miserable, so much so that he determined to commit suicide. He was down to the very dregs. Finally, one Sunday night as he made his way to the Embankment, determined to throw himself into the Thames and end it all, it suddenly 'occurred' to him to come into this building, and he came and sat in the gallery while I was leading in prayer. I did not know he was there, but I said something about God's love even to the backslider. I said it suddenly, without premeditation, not knowing anything. And what I said, though just an odd phrase, was a shaft of light from God to that poor soul. He came back to God and all is well with him. God's restoring grace! There he was walking the streets, when suddenly he felt the desire to come into the sanctuary. Why? Because God sent him in, God put the thought into his mind and he came in. God also put the thing I said into my mind and I uttered it in my prayer. I was in no sense responsible; I was quite unaware of it. That is how God works.

The history of the church is rich in such stories. Read Hugh Redwood's *God in the Slums* and *God in the Shadows*, or read *A Brand from the Burning* by Percy Rush. They are illustrations of the same thing, men and women converted but falling away, apparently gone right away for many years. How did Hugh Redwood himself come back? He was a journalist, and while collecting information about the flooding of the Thames in 1927 he again met with the Salvation Army. Some years before, he had been converted in the Salvation Army, but afterwards became a backslider. So, it may even take a flood to bring a child back to God. All these bear witness to God's restoring grace.

God brought these people back. Just when we have reached our limit, when we are most hopeless and when we are about to give way to final despair, when we are perhaps even driven to the thought of suicide, suddenly God intervenes, perhaps even at the last moment, and brings us back. He restores us to the fellowship – fellowship with himself most particularly, but also to the fellowship of his people, and gives us back the joy we had lost. He lifts us up out of 'the horrible pit, out of the miry clay' and sets our feet upon a rock and establishes our goings.

David, king of Israel, knew something about this. He had sinned so deeply that the only way God could deal with him was to send the prophet Nathan to him. And Nathan brought his sin home to him in the form of a parable, finally saying quite plainly, 'Thou art the man' (2 Samuel 12). Then David saw his guilt and that led to the writing of Psalm 51 and the confession of his sin. But he does not stop at this point. The Christian never stops at that point. Remorse can do that. It can make you condemn yourself and then, perhaps, commit suicide. But the Christian goes on and says with David, 'Wash me'; 'Restore unto me the joy of thy salvation.'

God's restoring grace. He brings the soul back again, according to his own wondrous love and his amazing kindness. We may sum up the doctrine like this. In the Christian life nothing is fortuitous; nothing happens or comes to pass by chance. Is there anything more consoling, more wonderful, than to know that we are in the hands of God? He controls everything. He is the Lord God Almighty, the Lord of the universe, who works everything according to the counsel of his own eternal will. He has set his love upon you; therefore nothing can harm you. 'The very hairs of your head are all numbered.' He will not let you go. You may fall deeply into sin, and go very far astray, but you will not be utterly cast down; he will hold you from that final fall. He will always bring you back. 'He restoreth my soul,' says the Psalmist. And after he restores he will lead you into 'green pastures' and by 'the still waters'. And he will deal with you in such a marvellous way that you will find it difficult to believe that you have ever done what you have done. God's restoring grace!

Is not our ignorance our main trouble? We talk so much about our decisions and what we are doing. We must learn to think in this other way and to see that it is God who has done it all. You never decided for Christ, it was he who laid his hand upon you and, to use Paul's term, 'apprehended' you. That is why you did decide. Go beyond your decision. What made you decide? Go back to the beginning, to the grace of God. It is all his grace, and if it were not, though you decided for Christ you would very soon decide otherwise, and you would fall right away and go right out. But you cannot fall from his grace. You can in your muddled intellect and thinking, but you cannot in fact. God's saving grace! But we need to be restrained afterwards, and when we fall we need to be restored. And he does it all. You must realize that 'it is God which worketh in you', from beginning to end. Thank God for his amazing grace – saving, restraining, wonderful restoring grace. 'Nevertheless I am still with thee.' It is almost incredible, but it is true. 'I am still with thee.'

Chapter Nine

THE FINAL PERSEVERANCE OF THE SAINTS

*Thou shalt guide me with thy counsel,
and afterward receive me to glory.*

In our last study we began to consider the biblical teaching concerning the grace of God as it is illustrated in the story of the writer of this Psalm. The general proposition is that salvation is entirely 'by grace . . . through faith; and that not of yourselves: it is the gift of God' (Ephesians 2:8). It is entirely grace. The glory is entirely God's for the salvation of every soul. Here we have the great formula of the Protestant Reformation which we must never forget. Then we found that the biblical teaching with respect to this can be thought of in certain categories. First, 'saving grace'. This is the original way in which grace comes to us, bringing forgiveness of sins. Then 'restraining grace'. We noticed that it was God who held this man back. His feet were almost gone. Why did he not slip? He thought it was the recollection of the harm he would be doing to the weaker brother. But the question is, Who put that into his mind? It was God. God restrains us. God allows his children to wander very far, so far at times that some people say, 'That man or that woman has never been a child of God.' But that, as we have seen, is to fail to understand the doctrine of backsliding. God seems to allow us to go a long way, but he never allows us to go all the way. He holds us by our right hand, he restrains us.

Then we saw the working of 'restoring grace'. God brought

this man back and took him to the sanctuary. It was not just an idle thought that entered his mind, causing him to say, 'Well, why not go to the house of God?' Anyone who has ever wandered away from God, reading these words, will, on examining his or her experience, find that what they thought had come as a sudden impulse was not a sudden impulse at all but God putting it into their mind. He manipulates our mind and thought. He had taken this man to the sanctuary and as a result he had restored him.

That is the point at which we have arrived. All that belongs to the past. The Psalmist is still, as it were, looking back. He cannot get over this, this 'nevertheless', this astonishing thing, 'I am still in the presence of God,' he says; 'God still looks on me and is concerned about me, God is still interested in me in spite of what I have been doing and in spite of what I almost did.' 'Nevertheless I am continually with thee.' He cannot get over it, and he says, 'I am here because of God and because of his grace.' And then, realizing that, he turns to the future. What is the future going to be like? His answer is, 'The future is going to be the same. I am continually in God's hand. Since "thou has holden me by my right hand", "thou shalt guide me with thy counsel, and afterward receive me to glory".'

The first point we must make here is that this further step that the Psalmist takes is one which is really quite inevitable in view of what he has already said. To me the whole case depends upon that proposition. My argument is that the person who has realized what the Psalmist has realized about the past must of necessity and by inevitable logic go on to say this about the future. So, if we cannot say what this man says about the future, it means there is a difficulty in our understanding of the past. In other words, the Christian life is a whole. The doctrine of grace is one and indivisible; you cannot take up parts of it and leave others. It is either all or none. So I say that this man goes on to make this statement because in a sense he is bound to do so. He argues like this, 'I have been restrained; I was held when I had almost gone, by the mighty hand of God. As a result of his grace, I am in the presence of God and now enjoy the presence of God. Why? Well, because of God's restoring grace. But now the question arises, Why has God dealt with me like this? Why did God restrain me? Why has God restored me? There is only one answer to that question. God has done this because I belong to him, because he is my Father, because I am his child. In other words, it is not something accidental or fortuitous. God has done this to me because of the relationship that exists between us, and therefore, if that is true, he must go on doing the same in the future.'

In other words, we are considering, whether we realize it or not, what is described as the doctrine of 'the final perseverance of the saints'. Are we familiar with this? There has been no doctrine brought to light by the Protestant Reformation which has given more joy and comfort and consolation to God's people. It was the doctrine that sustained the saints of the New Testament era as we shall see, and since that time there has been nothing that has so held and stimulated God's people. It explains some of the greatest exploits in the annals of the Christian church. You do not begin to understand people like the Covenanters of Scotland and the Puritans – people who gave up their lives and did so with a sense of joy and glory – except in the light of this doctrine. It is the explanation of some of the most amazing things that happened in the last war; it is the only way of understanding some of the German Christians who could face a Hitler and defy him.

Now the Psalmist gives us a remarkable statement of that doctrine. He turns to God and this is what he says, 'Thou shalt guide me with thy counsel, and afterward receive me to glory.' Many commentators have disagreed about the exact rendering of that. Some do not like the word 'afterward'. They say it should read, 'Thou shalt lead me after glory.' However, the meaning is one and the same. 'Afterward.' Whether we put these words in the present or the future there is a continuous element there. What he is saying is, 'You are doing this now, and you will go on doing this; and then "afterwards" – glory.' The man is not expressing a pious hope; he is absolutely certain, as the remainder of the Psalm explains at greater length and in detail.

This is a doctrine which is found throughout the Bible, in the Old Testament as well as in the New. The Old Testament saints all lived on earth in the light of it. It is the whole

181

explanation of the heroes of the faith mentioned in Hebrews 11 from Abel onward. It is seen particularly clearly in the case of Noah. Noah was a strange and foolish eccentric to the society in which he lived. He seemed so ridiculous, building an ark. He was not like the other people, living for this world. No, he was preparing for a catastrophe. And why did he do it? It was because he knew God and trusted him and desired to please him. There is a magnificent statement of the doctrine in Hebrews 11:13-16:

'These all died in faith, not having received the promises, but having seen them afar off, and were persuaded of them, and embraced them, and confessed that they were strangers and pilgrims on the earth. For they that say such things declare plainly that they seek a country. And truly, if they had been mindful of that country from whence they came out, they might have had opportunity to have returned. But now they desire a better country, that is, an heavenly: wherefore God is not ashamed to be called their God: for he hath prepared for them a city.'

That is a perfect summary of the way in which the Old Testament saints lived; it explains their faith and philosophy of life. It is a declaration of the doctrine of the final preservation of the saints. In the New Testament it is, as we should expect, very much clearer. And it is clearer for this good reason, that the Son of God has now been on earth and done his work, and therefore we should have a greater assurance than the Old Testament saints had. They had assurance, but we should be doubly sure. The Son of God has come down on earth and returned to heaven. He has been felt and touched and handled. We have all this evidence, and not only that, the Holy Spirit has been given in a way that was not experienced before Christ came. The effect of all this should be to make us doubly sure of this glorious and astounding doctrine of the final perseverance of the saints.

In considering this doctrine, we are looking at the truth about the backslider in a positive way. Previously, we looked at it in a negative way, considering the restraining and restoring aspects of God's grace. If now we put that in its positive form, and in the future, we have the doctrine of the perseverance of saints. Why does God not allow the backslider to go right away? Why do we say that the backslider always comes back and must come back? This doctrine provides the explanation.

Let us then look at this great doctrine. What evidence have we for it? This word in the Psalm which we are considering is one of the best. But listen to some of the statements in the New Testament. Listen to the words of the Lord Jesus Christ in John 10:28, 29:

'And I give unto them eternal life; and they shall never perish, neither shall any man pluck them out of my hand. My Father, which gave them me, is greater than all; and no man is able to pluck them out of my Father's hand.'

Now that statement in and of itself is more than enough. Those words were uttered by our blessed Lord and Saviour himself without any qualification. They are a dogmatic assertion, an absolute assurance. They could not be stronger. But consider also certain other passages of Scripture. Look at the end of Hebrews 6 and Hebrews 11. You may not be familiar with them, and there may be things about which you are not clear. But let me remind you of a great statement by Lord Bacon who said, 'Let not the things you are uncertain of rob you of that of which you are certain.' What a profound statement it is at any level. When applied to scriptural doctrines it means this. Here is a categorical statement made by our Lord which is clear and plain. There can be no equivocation about it; it is absolutely certain. Very well; when you come across other passages which seem to be uncertain, what do you do about them? Do you let go of the thing you are certain of? Lord Bacon says that, if you are wise, you must never let what you are uncertain about rob you of that which you are certain. What our Lord says is an absolute certainty, so you lay it down as an absolute proposition. Then you take the other verses and look at them in the light of this.

If you do that you will find that there is not much difficulty. As I pointed out before, in passing, in passages like the early verses in Hebrews 6 there is no statement to the effect that these people have been born again. Never forget that there are people who may appear to you to have become Christian, who subscribe to the right statements and who may appear to show many other signs, but it does not follow they are born-again Christians. They may have 'tasted' of the heavenly gift, they may have experienced something of the power of the Holy Spirit, but that does not mean of necessity they have received life from God. The doctrine of the perseverance of the saints applies only to those who have received life.

Consider now those repeated statements in Romans 8, and especially verse 30, 'Moreover whom he did predestinate, them he also called: and whom he called, them he also justified: and whom he justified, them he also glorified.' The apostle Paul teaches here quite plainly that if God has justified someone, he has already glorified that person. The whole of that portion of Scripture is but a tremendous exposition of the doctrine of the final perseverance of the saints ending with the ultimate challenge, 'Who shall separate us from the love of Christ?' and 'I am persuaded [and what a weak word that is; the Greek means 'I am certain', absolutely certain], that neither death, nor life, . . . shall be able to separate us from the love of God, which is in Christ Jesus our Lord.' Then take another one: 'He', says Paul to the Philippians (1:6), 'which hath begun a good work in you will perform it until the day of Jesus Christ.' Then go on to 1 Peter 1:5. The apostle says that we are 'kept by the power of God through faith unto salvation ready to be revealed in the last time'. And so on! We could spend hours just quoting Scripture to the same effect.

On the basis of these statements what exactly is this teaching? What are the truths which can be based upon these arguments? How do we prove, how do we demonstrate, this doctrine? It seems to me that the teaching can be sub-divided in the following manner.

This truth is based upon the unchanging character of God. 'The gifts and calling of God', said Paul, 'are without repentance.' He is 'the Father of lights, with whom is no variableness, neither shadow of turning'. God's will is an unchanging will, and it is an unchangeable will because God is God. What God wills, God does; what God purposes, God executes. The unchangeable will of God is the bed-rock of everything. If I do not believe that, I have no faith at all. It is an absolute truth that God is. 'I am that I am,' everlasting, unchangeable

184

and ever the same. In other words, God, unlike man, never starts a work only to give it up later on. That is so typical of us, is it not? We have our new interests and we live for them; and then we drop them. We all tend to be like that; but God is not like that. When God commences a work, God completes it. God is incapable of leaving anything half done. This is the bed-rock of our whole position. God never denies himself, he is never inconsistent. There are no contradictions in God, all is plain and clear. He sees the end from the beginning – that is God. If you do not rest on God's unchangeable will and purpose, you have nothing to rest upon at all.

The second argument I deduce concerns the purposes of God. Surely there is nothing clearer in the Scriptures from beginning to end than that God has a great purpose, and that his purpose is to save such as believe. You cannot read the Bible honestly and without prejudice without seeing that quite clearly. It gives you an account of creation, it gives you an account of the Fall and of mankind in sin. But then it introduces the message of grace. What is that? Is it not to display God's purpose to save such as believe? Now I am putting it like this deliberately. The Bible states clearly that there are certain people who are going to spend their eternity in glory, and that there are certain others who are not going to do so. If that is not the gospel, what is? You find it everywhere, this division, this judgment, this separation between God's people and those who are not God's people. It is God's purpose, I say, to save such as believe, and it is an unchanging purpose. It is a purpose that must be carried out. Why?

That brings me to my next argument which concerns the power of God. Now this world is governed by a power that is inimical to God. He is described as 'the god of this world' or 'Satan', and he has organized his forces with such unusual ability and power and subtlety that everything in this life and world is set against God's people. Temptations, suggestions, insinuations, the whole outlook, the whole bias – I need not describe them, they are all against us. And obviously the question that arises is this: Here is someone who is a child of God, how is he going to go through all this? Is he not certain to fall? Read the Old Testament and you will find

185

these godly people falling into sin, among them David, and many others. How can I be certain and sure that I can go on? The answer is that I am held by the power of God, sustained by this grace of God – 'Thou hast holden me by my right hand.' That is the only basis – the power of God. Of course it is a power which is invincible, illimitable and endless. That is why the apostle Paul, in praying for the church at Ephesus, prays three things for them (see Ephesians 1:18, 19). He prays that they 'may know what is the hope of his calling'. He prays that they may know what is 'the riches of the glory of his inheritance in the saints', and also 'what is the exceeding greatness of his power to us-ward who believe', even the power whereby he brought again, from the dead, our Lord Jesus Christ. 'Now,' says Paul in effect to these Ephesians, 'that is what I am praying for you. You are Christians in a pagan society and you are having a terrible time. The greatest thing you can ever know is this, that the power that is working in you is the power that God exercised when he brought his Son out from among the dead and raised him again.' That is the power that is working for us, in us. You see he is not content with saying it once, he repeats it, he emphasizes it. God's power is of such a type that he 'is able to do exceeding abundantly above all that we ask or think, according to the power that worketh in us' (Ephesians 3:20).

But I have an argument which is much more powerful than all I have said. I have something that is of even greater practical worth to you and me than the doctrines of the will of God and the purpose of God and the power of God. We are so dull of hearing, and we are so slow in spiritual things that these propositions may seem to us remote and abstract. I will therefore give you some concrete evidence in history, a practical demonstration of what I have been saying. We find it in the remainder of what this man says in verse 24 of this Psalm. I began by saying that he faces the future and that he does so in terms of what he deduces from the past. He does it quite logically. He says that the God who has dealt so graciously with him cannot possibly forsake him. But let me put that in its New Testament dress. This is how Paul puts it. 'If [I like that 'if', I like the logic of the New Testament], when we were enemies, we were reconciled to God by the death of his Son, much more, being reconciled, we shall be saved by his life' (Romans 5:10). Can you refute that logic? You see what he is saying. If this almighty God sent his only-begotten beloved Son to die upon the cross on Calvary's hill for us while we were enemies, how much more shall we be saved by his life? The God who has done that for us cannot leave us now. He would be denying himself were he to do so. Having done the greater he cannot refuse to do the lesser. He must.

But the apostle, knowing us, repeats it again in Romans 8:32, 'He that spared not his own Son, but delivered him up for us all, how shall he not with him also freely give us all things? He did not spare his humiliation; he did not spare his suffering; he did not spare the spitting and the cruel crown of thorns and the agony of the nails hammered into his holy hands and feet; he did not spare him the full blast of his wrath against sin. 'He that spared not his own Son . . . how shall he not with him also freely give us all things?' Do you want anything further? If that is not enough for you, I despair. The God who has done that for us is bound to give us everything that is essential for our final salvation. It is unthinkable that he should not do so. Our labour is never in vain in the Lord if we believe what Paul says in 1 Corinthians 15. And if that is true of our labour, how much more is it true of his labour.

Let me give you one last argument. The very way in which we are saved is final proof, it seems to me, of the doctrine of the final perseverance of the saints. What do I mean? I mean that we are saved by our union with Christ. That is the teaching of Romans 5 and 6. If you are ever in Christ and joined to him, you can never cease to be so. You become indissolubly part of him, you are united with Christ. The doctrine of justification proves it in the same way. God says, 'Their sins and iniquities will I remember no more.' We died with Christ; we were crucified with Christ; we have been buried with Christ; we have risen with Christ; we are seated with him in the heavenly places. All that is true of him is true of us. Can that ever cease to be? The doctrine of the rebirth teaches the same thing. We are partakers of the divine nature.

Adam was not. Adam was given a positive righteousness, but he was not a partaker of the divine nature. He was made in the image and likeness of God and no more; but the person who is in Christ, the person who is a Christian, the person who is born again is a 'partaker of the divine nature'. Christ is in him and he is in Christ.

Work out the logic of these propositions. If you believe those doctrines you will see that certain things follow inevitably. I cannot understand people who say that someone can be born again today but that tomorrow he may cease to be born again. It is impossible, it is monstrous, it is almost blasphemy to suggest it. You can have emotional experiences that come and go; you can take decisions and then renounce them. But the Bible teaches the activity and the action of God. And when God does a work it is done effectually; and if you are in Christ you are in Christ. If you are a partaker of the divine nature and joined to, and made a part of, Christ in spiritual union, there can be no severance.

There, then, are the arguments to prove and substantiate this doctrine. There now remains the question of how God does it. How does God sustain us? The Psalmist puts it like this, 'Thou shalt guide me with thy counsel.' He leads; he guides. He does all the things which we were considering in our previous study. He restrains us, he works within us – 'work out your own salvation with fear and trembling. For it is God which worketh in you both to will and to do' (Philippians 2:12f.) That is how he preserves his people; that is how he sustains us by his grace; that is how he delivers us from sin. He works in us, in our minds as well as in our dispositions and desires. Peter, at the beginning of the Second Epistle, reminds the people to whom he is writing that they have been given 'all things that pertain unto life and godliness'. 'All things' – everything that is necessary to live a godly life is given to us in the Scriptures, in the Holy Spirit, in the Person of Christ. By means of these things God leads us, and sustains us, he holds and perfects us. He is dealing with us. We are his workmanship and his chisel is used upon us. You have been ill? It may have been God doing it. 'For this cause many are weak and sickly among you', says Paul in 1 Corinthians 11:30. Because some of the members of the

church at Corinth had not been examining and judging themselves, God had had to deal with them through sickness and
illness. 'Whom the Lord loveth he chasteneth, and scourgeth
every son whom he receiveth' (Hebrews 12:6). That is often
a part of his process in sustaining us and bringing us to that
ultimate glorification that awaits us.

Let me end with this. What does all this process lead to?
According to this man it leads to 'glory'. 'Thou shalt' – and
if you prefer the other translation – 'thou shalt . . . lead me
on after glory.' It means that if we are thus in God's hands,
and are being sustained by him, we arrive at a certain amount
of glory even here in this world. Even in this world we begin
to enjoy something of the fruits of salvation, of the life that
is glory. The gifts of the Spirit, the graces of the Spirit, the
fruit of the Spirit – that is all part of the glory. When God
begins to produce these things in you he is glorifying you.
He makes you unlike the world and its people; he makes you
like Christ. Something of the glory of the blessed Lord
belongs to you. As Isaac Watts reminds us:

> *The men of grace have found*
> *Glory begun below;*
> *Celestial fruits on earthly ground*
> *From faith and hope may grow.*

> *The hill of Zion yields*
> *A thousand sacred sweets,*
> *Before we reach the heavenly fields*
> *Or walk the golden streets.*

Thank God it is true. Yes, but that is only the beginning;
that is only the foretaste. It is, indeed, only after death that
we shall arrive perfectly at the glory that awaits us, and enjoy
all that is meant by heaven. 'A crowning day is coming,
by and by.' '. . . There is laid up for me a crown of
righteousness . . .' says the great apostle Paul. That is why
he prays again and again for the churches that they might
know 'the hope of his calling', and 'the riches of the glory of
his inheritance in the saints'. In other words, God is preparing
us for himself, and the ultimate end of salvation is that we
go to be with God and enjoy God's life with him. What

poor creatures we are, what foolish creatures, grumbling and complaining, holding on to the things of this world. Do you know that you and I, if we are in Christ, are destined to enjoy the life and the glory of God himself? That is the glory that awaits us. It is not merely forgiveness of sins; we are being prepared for that positive, eternal glory. That is the teaching this Psalmist goes on to expound. That is the end and the objective to which God's sustaining grace is leading us, and for which he is preparing us.

But I imagine someone saying, 'Is not this rather dangerous doctrine? Is there not a danger that someone may say, "Well, as I am saved, it does not matter what I do"?' My reply is this. If you can listen to the doctrine I have been enunciating and draw that deduction, then you have no spiritual life in you – you are dead. 'Every man that hath this hope in him', says John in 1 John 3:3, 'purifieth himself, even as he is pure.' If you were promised an audience with some great person, you would prepare yourself for it. And what I have been telling you is that if you are a child of God you are going to be ushered into the eternal presence and you will stand before the glory of God. 'Blessed are the pure in heart: for they shall see God.' The more certain I am of that, the more concerned shall I be about my sanctification and purity, and the more I shall purify myself. The time is short. I know that the end is coming; I have not a moment to lose. I must prepare with more and more diligence for 'the crowning day' that is coming 'by and by'.

I end then with a piece of logic from John Newton. He worked it out like this:

> *His love in time past forbids me to think*
> *He'll leave me at last in trouble to sink:*
> *Each sweet Ebenezer I have in review,*
> *Confirms his good pleasure to help me quite through.*

God grant that we all, as we look back at our past 'Ebenezers' (see 1 Samuel 7:12), may enjoy this glorious, blessed certainty that he cannot, he will not forsake us. We are certain – blessed be the name of God –

The soul that on Jesus has leaned for repose
He will not, he cannot, desert to its foes;
That soul, though all hell should endeavour to shake,
He never will leave, he will never forsake.

Chapter Ten

THE ROCK OF AGES

Whom have I in heaven but thee?
and there is none upon earth that I desire
* beside thee.*
My flesh and my heart faileth:
but God is the strength of my heart, and
* my portion for ever.*

In these words the Psalmist describes yet a further step in the
process of his recovery from the spiritual sickness from which
he had been suffering. We have followed him step by step,
and now he comes to this next stage, this further statement,
which, beyond any question, is the final position, the topmost
level of all. Here, in view of all his experience, he can do
nothing but give himself to the worship and adoration of
God. That is what he expresses in these two verses. 'Whom
have I in heaven but thee? and there is none upon earth that
I desire beside thee. My flesh and my heart faileth: but God
is the strength of my heart, and my portion for ever.'

This next step is quite inevitable, and I am very concerned
to emphasize that point. One of the most interesting things
about following this man in his spiritual pilgrimage has been
to notice the way each step is connected with the one before
and the one after. I would suggest that in this we have what
we may well describe as the normal spiritual experience. We
have remarked as we have been going along that if we stop
at any one of these positions there is something wrong with
us in a spiritual sense. He had arrested the downward progress
by that first stand, and from that very moment he began to

climb up from step to step and rung to rung. Each movement
was inevitable because an understanding of any one of these
situations must lead directly to the next. Thus, having realized
all these truths about God and his gracious dealing with him,
having gained this insight into the marvellous doctrine of
grace in its various manifestations, the Psalmist almost invol-
untarily and quite inevitably found himself worshipping God
and adoring him at his wonderful throne of grace. This, I
would repeat, is the end of the process, and it is the highest
level to which we can ever attain. Indeed, in these two verses
we see the goal of salvation. This is what it is all about, what
it is all for; and the Psalmist had arrived at it.

Let me digress for a moment at this point: one often finds
a tendency among Christian people to depreciate the Old
Testament. It is not that they do not believe in it as the Word
of God. They do. But they tend to contrast themselves with
the saints of the Old Testament. 'We are in Christ,' they say,
'we have received the Holy Spirit. The Old Testament saints
did not know of this and they are therefore inferior to us.'
If you are tempted to think like that I have one simple question to put to you: Can you honestly use the language that
this man uses in these two verses? Have you arrived at a
knowledge of God and an experience of God such as this
man had? Can you say quite honestly, 'Whom have I in
heaven but thee? and there is none upon earth that I desire
beside thee'? How prejudiced we are. These Old Testament
saints were children of God as you and I are; indeed, if we
read these Psalms quite honestly we shall at times feel rather
ashamed of ourselves, and occasionally begin to wonder
whether they had not gone farther than we have ever gone.
Let us be careful lest we press the difference between the two
dispensations too far and make distinctions which end by
being thoroughly unscriptural.

This is how the Psalmist can speak of his relationship to
God, and I do not hesitate to aver that the whole business of
the New Testament gospel and its salvation is simply to bring
us to this. This is the test of Christian profession; this is the
whole purpose of the incarnation and the entire work of our
blessed Lord and Saviour – to enable us to speak like this. I
would ask again, therefore: Can we speak like this? Is this

our experience? Do we know God as this man knew him? Whatever else we may have, whatever else we may be able to say, we must never be satisfied until we can come to this. This is the goal, this is the objective. To be satisfied with anything short of this, however good, is in a sense to deny the gospel itself, for the great and grand end and object of the whole gospel is to bring us, as we shall see, to this particular position.

Let us then face this tremendous statement, 'Whom have I in heaven but thee? and there is none upon earth that I desire beside thee. My flesh and my heart faileth: but God is the strength of my heart, and my portion for ever.' What does he mean? What is he saying? I am sure the first thing in his mind was a negative and that he was making a negative statement. By his very question he is saying that, as the result of his experience, he has found that there is no-one else anywhere who can help him, that nowhere is there any other Saviour. 'Who is there who can help me in heaven or earth but thou?' he asks. There is no-one else. When things have gone wrong, when he is really at the end of his tether, when he does not know where to go or to whom to turn, when he needs comfort and solace and strength and assurance, and something to hold on to, he has found that there is no-one apart from God.

Now his negative is important for us all. Indeed, I thank God for that negative because I find it very comforting. For I imagine that what this man is saying is that, despite his imperfections, despite his failure, when he was away from God, and more or less turning his back upon him, he could find no satisfaction. In his experience, when he was wrong with God he was wrong everywhere. There was an emptiness about his life – no satisfaction, no blessing, no strength – and even though he was not able to make any positive statement about God, he could at least say there was nothing and no-one else! Now that is a very comforting thought. Are we able to use this negative, I wonder? If we are afraid of the positive test, how do we stand with this negative test? Can we say that we have seen through everything in this life and world? Have we yet come to see that everything that the world offers is a 'broken cistern'? Have we really been enabled to see through the world and its ways and all its supposed glory? Have we come to the point where we can say: Well, I know this much at any rate; there is nothing else that can satisfy me. I have tried what the world has to offer, I have experimented with all those things, I have played with them and I have come to this conclusion, that when I am away from God, to quote Othello, 'chaos is come again'.

This is an important aspect of experience, and a very vital one. Anyone who has been a backslider knows exactly what I am saying. It is one of the ways of proving my previous remarks about the backslider. The backslider is someone who, because of his relationship to God, can never really enjoy anything else. He may try, but he is miserable while it lasts. He has seen through it. This, therefore, is something by which we may always test ourselves. In a remarkable way we have in this confession a striking test of our Christian faith and belief. That is often the first step in our recovery – a realization that everything has actually become different, 'old things are passed away; behold, all things are become new'. Things of the world do not seem to possess the charm and value they once seemed to have. We discover that when we are not in the right relationship to God the very foundations seem to have gone. We may travel to the ends of the earth in an attempt to find satisfaction without God. But we find that there is none.

But obviously we do not stop there with the negative. This statement is also a very positive one. Let me emphasize this by analysing this man's positive assertion. He is saying in the first place that he now desires God himself, not only what God gives or what he does. Now that is a most important statement, for this reason. The whole essence of the Psalmist's problem, in a sense, was that he had put what God gives in the place of God himself. That was what underlay his problem concerning the ungodly. They were having a good time, so why was he having such a bad time? Why had he been plagued all the day long? Why was it that he seemed to have cleansed his heart and washed his hands in innocency in vain? Why was it he thought like this? His trouble was that he was more interested in the things that God gives than in God himself, and because he did not seem to be having the things he wanted, he began to doubt God's love. But now he has come to the place in which he can say quite honestly that he desires God himself as God, and not only what God gives and what God does.

Let me put this as strongly as possible. The ultimate test of the Christian is that he can truly say that he desires God even more than he desires forgiveness. We all desire forgiveness, and rightly so; but that is a very low state of Christian experience. The height of Christian experience is when we can say, 'Yes, but beyond forgiveness what I desire is God, God himself.' We often desire power, and ability, and various other gifts. There is a sense in which it is right to desire them. But if we ever put those things before God, again we are proclaiming that we are very poor Christians. As Christians we desire blessings of various types and pray to God for them, but in doing so we may sometimes be insulting God in a sense, because we imply that we are not interested in him but in the fact that he is able to give us these blessings. We desire the blessings and we do not stop to enjoy the blessed Person himself. This man had been through all that, and now has come to see that the greatest of all blessings is just to know God and to be in his presence.

There are many examples of this in the Bible. Psalm 42:1, 2 expresses it perfectly, 'As the hart panteth after the water brooks, so panteth my soul after thee, O God.' That man is crying out for this direct knowledge of God, this immediate experience of God. His soul 'panteth', he is 'thirsting' for him, the living God. Not God as an idea, not God as a source and fount of blessing, but the living Person himself. Do we know this? Do we hunger for him and thirst for him? Are our souls panting after him? This is a very profound matter, and the terrible thing is that it is possible to go through life praying day by day and yet never realizing that the supreme point in Christian experience is to come face to face with God, to worship him in the Spirit and in a spiritual manner. Do we know that we are doing business and having dealings directly with the living God? Have we known his presence? Is he real to us? Or let me put it on a lower level. Are we longing for and seeking that? Are we without satisfaction until we have it? Is the greatest desire of our hearts and our

197

highest ambition, beyond all other blessings and experiences, just to know that we are there before him and that we know him and are enjoying him? That is what the Psalmist desires in the Psalm 42: that is what this Psalmist of ours in Psalm 73 was actually enjoying.

The apostle Paul says exactly the same thing in Philippians 3:10. 'If you ask me,' says Paul, 'what my greatest desire is, it is this: "That I may know him." ' You notice his supreme ambition. Let me not be misunderstood as I put it plainly. His supreme ambition was not to be a great soul winner. That was one ambition of his, and a right one. It was not even to be a great preacher. No, beyond it all, including it all, 'That I may know him.' Because, as the apostle reminds us elsewhere, if you put the other things first you may find yourself, even as a preacher, becoming, in a sense, a castaway. But when we put Paul's desire at the centre there is no danger. Paul had seen the face of the living Christ, the risen Lord. Yet what he hungers for and pants after is this further, deeper, more intimate knowledge of him, a personal knowledge, a personal revelation of the living Lord in a spiritual sense.

There is nothing higher than this. Look at the aged John writing his farewell letter to Christians. His great desire, he tells them in 1 John 1:4, is 'that your joy may be full'. How is it to be full? 'That ye also may have fellowship with us', that you may share with us as partners the blessed experience we enjoy. And what is that? 'Our fellowship is with the Father, and with his Son Jesus Christ.' It does not just mean that you are engaged in God's work. It means that, of course; but that is the lowest level. The highest level is really to know God himself. 'This is life eternal, that they might know thee the only true God, and Jesus Christ, whom thou hast sent' (John 17:3). Indeed, we have the authority of our Lord himself, not only in the statement I have just quoted but in another statement. When a man asked him which was the greatest commandment of all, he said, 'Thou shalt love the Lord thy God with all thy heart, and with all thy soul, and with all thy mind. . . . And the second is like unto it, Thou shalt love thy neighbour as thyself' (Matthew 22:37, 39). The first thing, the most important thing in life, is that we so know God that we love him with the whole of our being. To be satisfied with anything short of that, or with anything less than that is to misunderstand the whole end and object and purpose of Christian salvation. Do not stop at forgiveness. Do not stop at experiences. The end is to know God, and nothing less. This Psalmist is able to say that he now desires God for his own sake, and not merely for what God gives and does.

Now let me put it another way. This man not only desires God himself, he desires nothing but God. He is exclusive in his desire. He elaborates that. He says first that he desires nothing in heaven but God. What a statement. 'Whom have I in heaven but thee?' May I ask another question – and I think it is these simple questions that really tell us the whole truth about ourselves. What are you looking for and hoping for in heaven? Let me ask a question that perhaps should come before that. Do you ever look forward to being in heaven? That is not being morbid. I like the way in which Matthew Henry put it: 'We are never told in the Scriptures that we should look forward to death; but we are told very frequently that we should look forward to heaven.' The person who looks forward to death simply wants to get out of life because of his troubles. That is not Christian; that is pagan. The Christian has a positive desire for heaven, and therefore I ask: Do we look forward to being in heaven? But, more than this, what do we look forward to when we get to heaven? What is it we are desiring? Is it the rest of heaven? Is it to be free from trouble and tribulations? Is it the peace of heaven? Is it the joy of heaven? All those things are to be found there, thank God; but that is not the thing to look forward to in heaven. It is the face of God. 'Blessed are the pure in heart: for they shall see God.' The Vision Splendid, the *Summum Bonum*, to stand in the very presence of God – 'To gaze and gaze on thee.' Do we long for that? Is that heaven to us? Is that the thing we want above everything else? It is the thing to covet and to long for.

The apostle Paul tells us that to die is 'to be with Christ'. There is no need to add anything to that. That is why, I believe, we are told so little in a detailed sense about the life in heaven and in glory. People often ask why we are not told more about it. I think there are two answers to that. One is that because of our sinful state any description we might be given would be misunderstood by us. It is so glorious that we can neither understand nor grasp it. The second reason is more important; it is that it is often idle curiosity that desires to know more. I will tell you what heaven is. It is 'to be with Christ', and if that does not satisfy you, then you do not know Christ at all. 'Whom have I in heaven but thee?' says the Psalmist. I do not want anything else. Where thou art is heaven. Just to look at thee is sufficient. 'To be with Christ' is more than enough, it is everything. 'Whom have I in heaven but thee?'

How much do we know of this experience? We have had certain experiences and blessings; there are certain things we know already; but this is the test: Do we know him, do we long for him? Just to be with him, to be conversing with him. Do we pant after him? Are we thirsting after the living God and for this intimacy with the Lord Jesus Christ? That is the real Christian experience. How much time do we spend with him, praying to him? 'Whom have I in heaven but thee?'

In the same way he goes on to say, 'There is none upon earth that I desire beside thee.' Again let us notice why the Psalmist says this. He says it because that was the very essence of his previous trouble. It was because he was desiring certain things that others had, that he had been in trouble. 'For I was envious at the foolish, when I saw the prosperity of the wicked. For there are no bands [no pangs] in their death: but their strength is firm.' And he had wanted to be like them and to have those things that they had: but now he no longer wants them. He has seen through all that. Now, 'there is none upon earth that I desire beside thee' – God alone in heaven, God alone on earth.

The Scripture, again, is full of like teaching. This is how our Lord puts it in Luke 14:26, 'If any man come to me, and hate not his father, and mother, and wife, and children, and brethren, and sisters, yea, and his own life also, he cannot be my disciple.' Do not worry about that word 'hate'; it is simply a strong word which makes it clear that anyone who puts anyone or anything in his life before Christ is not a true disciple of his. To be a true disciple of Christ means that Christ is at the centre, Christ is the Lord of my life, Christ

200

is on the throne of my being; it means that I love him first before everyone and everything. 'None upon earth that I desire beside thee.' Does he come first in our lives? Even before our loved ones and our nearest and dearest? Even before our work, before our success, before our business, before anything else while we are here on earth? He should be our supreme desire. 'To me to live . . .' is what? 'is Christ,' says St Paul. It is to be walking through this world with Christ himself, to be having fellowship with him in this life. And because this was true of him, he could also say that he had learned 'in whatsoever state I am, therewith to be content'. Why? Other things no longer control him. It is Christ, it is Christ alone he wants. If I have Christ, he says, I have all and 'I can do all things through Christ which strengtheneth me' (Philippians 4:11,13). We are independent of circumstances and surroundings when living in him and by him and for him, and all other things pale into insignificance. Do we desire him above everything else as we go through this earthly pilgrimage? The Psalmist had reached the point at which he could say that he did.

Not only that, he goes on to tell us that he finds complete satisfaction in God. The whole statement means that; but once more he expounds it for us in detail. 'Whom have I in heaven but thee? and there is none upon earth that I desire beside thee. My flesh and my heart faileth: but God is the strength of my heart, and my portion for ever.' His portion, that is it; his supply, his satisfaction, his everything. There is nothing that he can desire but God. And what is God? He is Sun and Shield, he gives grace and glory. There is no end to it. He finds that God satisfies him completely – his mind, his heart, his whole person. Do you find complete intellectual satisfaction in God and in his holy work? Do you get all your philosophy here and feel that you need nothing beyond it? God satisfies us completely, the heart, the affections also. He fills everything:

> *Ransomed, healed, restored, forgiven,*
> *Who like thee his praise should sing?*

God is all and in all. He is everything, my portion, my complete satisfaction. I desire nothing else, I want nothing

201

in addition. Read the Psalms and you will find that theme everywhere. In Psalm 103, for example, you will find that that is exactly what the Psalmist is saying: God healing his diseases and sicknesses, casting his sins from him as far as the east is from the west, giving him strength and power – everything. He is fully satisfied by this blessed, glorious God.

That brings us to the last point, which is that the Psalmist rests confidently in God. He desires God for himself, for his own sake rather than for what he gives. He desires nothing but God. He finds complete satisfaction in God, and he rests and reposes confidently in him. Listen to him, 'My flesh and my heart faileth: but God is the strength of my heart, and my portion for ever.' There are those who say that he is referring here not only to the time when his flesh would decay through age, but also to something he was experiencing at the time. Probably they are right, because you cannot pass through a spiritual experience such as this man passed through without your physical body suffering. I believe this man's nerves were in a bad state. His physical heart may have been misbehaving itself. 'My flesh and my heart faileth.' He may have been in a bad state physically. But in any case, looking to the future, he knows there is a day coming when his flesh and his heart will fail. He will become an old man; his faculties will fail; his strength will falter; he will not be able to feed himself; he will be lying helpless in his bed; things of time and earth will be slipping away. 'It will still be all right,' says this man, 'for whatever may happen God, the same yesterday, today and for ever, will still be the strength of my heart.'

It is generally agreed that the word which is translated 'strength' is the word 'rock'. 'But God is the Rock of my heart, and my portion for ever.' I rather like that, because it conjures up an image in our minds. 'O, yes,' says this man, 'I know that I am in such a position that I can rest quietly and confidently in him. I know that I can say that, even though a day may come when I shall feel the foundations of life shaking beneath me, God will be a rock that will hold me. He cannot be moved; he cannot be shaken. He is the Rock of ages, and wherever I am, and whatever may be happening, however my physical frame is behaving, and even when the things of earth are passing away, God the Rock will sustain me and I shall never be moved. 'God is the Rock, the strength, of my heart, and my portion for ever.'

The Bible is never tired of saying this. Read what others say. Whatever terrible conditions may come to pass, this is the comfort and consolation that they all give. Not only is God a Rock but 'underneath are the everlasting arms'. Your foundations in life may be gone, everything you built on may be crashing down and you yourself going down into the abyss. But, no; 'underneath' – and they are always there – 'underneath are the everlasting arms'. They are always holding you; you will never finally crash; you will be held when everything else is gone. Listen to Isaiah stating the same thing. He talks about that 'foundation stone'; that 'tried stone . . . a sure foundation' that has been set, and what he says is, 'He that believeth shall not make haste.' A better translation is that given in the New Testament, 'He that believeth on him shall not be confounded.' Or according to another possible translation, 'He that believeth shall never be put to shame.' Why not? He is on the Rock, he has this support, he has this foundation, and it cannot be moved, for it is God himself. And on this Rock, though my flesh and my heart may fail, I shall never be moved, I shall never be taken by surprise, I shall never be put to shame. God will see me right through.

Let me try to sum it up in a hymn which is the final confession of the Christian:

> *My hope is built on nothing less*
> *Than Jesus' blood and righteousness;*
> *I dare not trust my sweetest frame,*
> *But wholly lean on Jesus' name.*
> > *On Christ, the solid Rock, I stand;*
> > *All other ground is sinking sand.*
>
> *When darkness seems to veil his face,*
> *I rest on his unchanging grace;*
> *In every high and stormy gale*
> *My anchor holds within the veil.*
>
> *His oath, his covenant, and blood,*
> *Support me in the 'whelming flood;*

> *When all around my soul gives way,*
> *He then is all my hope and stay.*

Do you know this? Are you on the Rock? Do you know him? Do not try to live on your family; do not live on your business, or on your own activity; do not live on your experiences, or anything else. They will all come to an end and the devil will suggest that even your highest experiences can be explained psychologically. Let us live on nothing, let us trust nothing, but him. He is the Rock of ages, the everlasting God:

> *On Christ, the solid Rock, I stand;*
> *All other ground is sinking sand.*

Chapter Eleven

THE NEW RESOLUTION

For, lo, they that are far from thee shall
  perish:
thou hast destroyed all them that go a
  whoring from thee,
But it is good for me to draw near to
  God:
I have put my trust in the Lord God,
that I may declare all thy works.

These closing verses summarize the conclusion at which the Psalmist arrived as the result of the experience which he describes in detail in the rest of the Psalm. They represent his final meditation, and take the form of a resolution. He has finished his review of the past, and is facing himself and the future. He resolves that, as far as he is concerned, there is one thing he is going to do, whatever else he may not do. 'Nearness to God is good for me,' he says. 'This is the thing on which I am going to concentrate.'

In putting it like this the Psalmist gives us an insight into what had become his whole philosophy of life, his way of facing the uncertainties that lay ahead of him. It is here that we discover the great value of the Psalms. These men not only related their experiences in this world, they also recorded their reactions to them, and as the result of all that had happened to them they propounded certain great principles. We have here, therefore, the quintessence of their wisdom. Divine, heavenly wisdom is to be found in the Bible, and in a sense this man's ultimate conclusion is simply the great central message of the Bible. It tells us that in the last analysis there are only two possible views of life and only two possible ways of life.

We can do nothing better, then, as we conclude our studies of this great Psalm, than to consider this man's wisdom. Each one of us has arrived at a certain stage in life; we have all had various experiences. I wonder whether we have arrived at the same conclusion as the Psalmist? I wonder whether we see that this is really the essence of wisdom? I wonder, as we face our unknown future, whether we are facing it in this same way?

Let us begin by looking at the actual resolution which the Psalmist had formed. Here it is again in the Authorized Version, 'But it is good for me to draw near to God.' Another translation could be this, 'But as for myself, nearness to God is good for me.' He is contrasting himself with others. Whatever may be true about them, it is nearness to God that is good for him. His chief ambition is going to be just that, to keep near to God. He helps us to see the importance of this resolution by putting it in the form of a contrast. 'For, lo,' he says, 'they that are far from thee shall perish: . . . but it is good for me to draw near to God.' There are only these two positions in this life. We are all either far from God or near to him. And there is no other possible position, so that it is vitally important that we should arrive at this man's resolve, to be near to God.

I have no doubt at all but that what was uppermost in his mind was something like this. Reviewing his sad experience he came to the conclusion that what had really been wrong with him, and what had accounted for all his trouble, was just the fact that he did not keep near to God. He had thought it was the fact that the ungodly seemed to prosper while he experienced nothing but troubles. But now, having been given the enlightenment which he had in the sanctuary of God, he sees quite clearly that this was not the root cause of his trouble at all. There is only one thing that matters and that is man's relationship to God. If I am near to God, says this man, it does not really matter what happens to me; but if I am far from God, nothing can eventually be right. And this is the very profound conclusion to which he came.

We all tend to think that we need certain things. We think that our happiness depends upon conditions and events. Now it was because he had been thinking in that way that the Psalmist had got into such a wretched condition. The very sight of the ungodly and their apparent prosperity had upset him, and had made him envious, and he had begun to grumble and complain. He had spent days and weeks in that wretched state of self-pity, and he now sees that it was due entirely to the fact that he had not kept near to God. This is the beginning and the end of wisdom in the Christian life. The moment we move away from God everything goes wrong. The one secret is to keep near to God. When we fail, we are like a ship at sea that loses sight of the North star, or whose compass fails. If we lose our bearings, we must not be surprised at the consequences. That is what this man discovered. 'This is what I need,' he says, 'not blessings, not the prosperity other people have, not these other things of which the world makes so much. The one thing that matters is to be near to God, because while I was far away from him everything went wrong and I was wretched; but now that I have come back, though my conditions remain the same, all is well with me, I am full of joy and peace, I can rest confidently and happily and securely in the arms of his love. Therefore, this is my resolution. For myself, I am going to live near to God. That is always going to be the big thing in my life. I am going to start with that every day as it comes. I am going to say to myself, whatever else happens, that this is the essential thing, to be near to God.'

—Now that was the Psalmist's resolution and, fortunately for us, he also lets us into the secret of why he arrived at this resolution. We should thank God more and more for the Bible and its detailed instruction. The Bible never gives us just a general injunction; it always gives us reasons for it. And we need them, for we easily forget the general injunction. Here are some that are suggested in these two verses.

One good reason for keeping near to God is the contemplation of the fate of those who do not do so. He puts that first, you notice, and I think that he does so because he is still, in a sense, thinking experimentally. It was these ungodly people who really had led him astray. He is anxious, therefore, to safeguard himself against falling into that trap again. He knows, as he comes to face the future, that the world is not going to change. The ungodly will still be as they have always been, their eyes 'standing out with fatness'. Everything may be marvellous and wonderful for them. But he is never again going to fall into the trap. So he puts it first. 'Lo,' he says, 'they that are far from thee shall perish: thou hast destroyed all them that go a whoring from thee.' God has done it in the past, he will do it in the future.

Now we have been through all this in detail. The Psalmist has dealt with it at length. 'Surely thou didst set them in slippery places: thou castedst them down into destruction. How are they brought into desolation, as in a moment! they are utterly consumed with terrors.' 'Then understood I their end'! That is just a summary of history. That is the whole story of the world before the Flood and after, the whole story of Sodom and Gomorrah and similar events in history. What a fool Abraham seemed, wandering among the mountains with his sheep, in contrast with Lot's prosperous situation in the cities of the plain, with their vice and immorality. Well might he have asked: Does it pay to be godly? 'But lo,' he also might have said, 'they that are far from thee shall perish: thou hast destroyed all them that go a whoring from thee.' That is the long story of Old Testament history put here very plainly, 'They that are far from thee shall perish.'

If you take your view of life from the newspapers you may well think that the non-Christian world is having a marvellous time with its glittering prizes, its pomp and glory and wealth. But it does not matter what the temporary prosperity of the ungodly may be; although at this moment all appearances may be to the contrary it is as certain as the fact that we are alive that those who are far from God shall perish. 'The mills of God grind slowly,' very slowly, and at times we think they are not moving at all, 'yet they grind exceeding small.' That is the message of the Bible from beginning to end. That is what the life of faith means. We are all called to view life in the way the great heroes of the faith mentioned in Hebrews 11 viewed it. We have to do what Moses did. We have to esteem the reproach of Christ greater riches than the treasures in Egypt; we have to see through this world and its life; we have to see it under condemnation, under the wrath of God; we have to see the punishment that is most surely coming to it. It is all going to perish, it is passing away. We must therefore see through its vanity, its emptiness, its nothingness. Then we shall resolve, as this man resolved, to keep near to God. The world and its works are all passing away – 'change and decay in all around I see'; moth and rust are in the very warp and woof of the most glittering, golden prizes that the world can offer. We must realize that we are moving steadily in the direction of the grand assize, the end of the world, the last judgment. 'They that are far from thee shall perish.'

Are we clear about that, I wonder? Is our worship of God grudging, is there any hesitation in our mind as we face the future, as to whether we should go on with the Christian life? Are we somewhat shaken as we look around and see others who seem to have the best of everything – people who never go to a place of worship but with whom nothing ever seems to go wrong? Is the Bible true?

We need to learn the lesson that was taught to a farmer by an old minister in America. This farmer decided one particularly wet summer that he would harvest his crops on a Sunday. The old minister warned him and others like him against this. But this man decided he would do it, and he had marvellous crops and his barns were bulging. He said to the old minister, when he met him on one occasion, that his preaching must be wrong. 'Sudden calamity has not descended upon me,' he said; 'my barns have not caught fire; God has not killed one of my children or robbed me of my wife. Yet I have done the thing you always warned me not to do because of the consequences that would follow. But nothing has happened. What about your preaching now?' The old minster looked at the farmer and replied, 'God does not always make up his accounts in the fall.' He does not always do it at once. But as certainly as we are here in this world now, this is the message of the Bible, 'They that are far from God shall perish.' There is nothing else for them. It may take a long time, appearances may all be to the contrary, but it is certain, it is sure. There is no gospel apart from this. What is the message of the gospel? 'Flee from the wrath to come,' and if there is no 'wrath' there is no need of a salvation. That is the first reason for his resolution. I have no interest in a so-called gospel which does away with the fear of hell. There are wonderful people who say that they are not interested in hell or in heaven, but believe in doing good for its own sake. But the Bible warns us against hell, and it shows us the glory of heaven.

But the second reason is more positive. Here, this man puts it in terms of the character of God. 'It is good for me to draw near to God: I have put my trust in the Lord God.' He has resolved to be near to God and to live his life as near to God as possible. Why? Because God is good, because of the character of God.

Here again, I am sure, we all feel condemned because this element enters so little into our religious life and worship. If we but realized the true character of God there would be nothing we should desire in this world more than to be in the presence of God. We desire to be in the presence of people we like and love. We like to be introduced to, and to be in the presence of, people who are considered great in various ways and for various reasons. And yet how loath we are to spend our time in the presence of God. How ready we are to think of God as the mere distributor of blessings, and how slow we are to realize the glory of being in his presence. The Lord God, the Lord, Jehovah! That is what this man calls him. He is emphasizing the sovereignty of God, the unutterable greatness and majesty of God. The Lord God Almighty, the Creator of the heavens and of the earth, the self-existent God, the Eternal God, the Absolute, the Everlasting God – He is the One to whom we can draw near.

Another truth he emphasizes particularly by using the name Jehovah, is God as the covenant God, God if you like, in his covenant relationship to human beings. You remember that it was especially when God called Moses to deliver the Children of Israel out of captivity and the bondage of Egypt that he gave a special revelation of himself as Jehovah. He had given his name before, but at this point he defined it; and he always uses this name when the covenant is involved. In other words, God in his gracious purpose towards us, God as the God who planned salvation, God as the God who is concerned about our well-being, our welfare and happiness, covenants himself, pledges himself to us, that he is going to do all this for us. Now, says the Psalmist, the one thing I want in life above everything else is to keep near to such a God. I want to keep in touch with him. That is how we would put it. We are grateful to some great personage when he says that he is going to keep in touch with us. And we like to keep in touch with such people. We feel it is a privilege and an honour, and rightly so. But would that we might see that the ultimate blessing of the salvation which the Lord Jesus Christ came to give us is eternal life.

What is eternal life? Our Lord has defined it. 'This is life eternal, that they might know thee the only true God, and Jesus Christ, whom thou hast sent' (John 17:3). Or, as John puts it in his First Epistle, where he writes in order that his readers 'may have fellowship with us: and truly our fellowship is with the Father, and with his Son Jesus Christ' (1 John 1:3). Now the Psalmist says, 'This is my resolve. I want to keep near this God; I want to keep in touch with him; I want to spend all my time with him; I want to live as always in his presence. I like to think of his power and his promises, to remember his constancy.' And is not this a comforting and consoling, as well as an uplifting, thought? We do not know what is awaiting us, we live in a world that is full of change and we ourselves are inconsistent. The best of us are changeable creatures. And there is nothing so characteristic of our world as its instability and uncertainty. Is there anything more wonderful than to know that, at any moment, we can enter into the presence of One who is everlastingly the same, 'the Father of lights, with whom is no variableness, neither shadow of turning' (James 1:17)? Whatever may be happening around us, whatever may be happening inside us, we can go to One who is always the same, the same in his might, his majesty, his glory, his love, his mercy, his compassion, and the same in all that he has promised! Do you not understand this man now? 'I do not care about the others,' he says; 'but I, as for me, nearness to God is good for me.' Let us think more about God. Let us meditate upon him; let us turn our minds and our hearts towards him. Let us realize that in Christ he offers us his fellowship, his companionship, and that constantly and always.

There is yet a further reason here. 'It is good for me,' he says; 'nearness to God is good for me.' Now I have already emphasized this, and I want to re-emphasize it. The pragmatic element must never be excluded. I mean by that, not that we become Christians in order to derive certain blessings, but that if we are Christians we shall receive certain blessings. And it is right that we should remember this. It was 'for the joy that was set before him' that our blessed Lord 'endured the cross'; and is not this what the apostle means when he says, 'I reckon that the sufferings of this present time are not worthy to be compared with the glory which shall be revealed in us' (Romans 8:18)? Put these things in the right order. Start with God as God, and because he is God, and then remember that he is God for you. In other words, it means that being near to God is the place of salvation. And that is why the Psalmist wants to remain there. It is not surprising that he says that it is good for him to draw near to God in view of the experience he had gone through. You remember his misery and wretchedness and how it was too painful for him until he went into the sanctuary of God. But there, having understood the position, his happiness came flooding back to him. He rejoiced in God, and he felt that he had never been so happy in the whole of his life, though the circumstances of the ungodly were still the same. It is good to keep near to God; it is the place of salvation and deliverance.

James in his practical manner puts this very simply in his Epistle. 'Draw nigh to God,' he says, 'and he will draw nigh to you' (James 4:8). This, again, is a glorious thought, and we can be certain that every time we take a step in the direction of God – if I may speak thus – God will take a step in our direction. Do not imagine when you consider drawing near to God that you will find it difficult. If we approach him truly, if we approach him honestly, we can always be certain that God will meet us. He is the God of salvation. That is a very good reason for drawing near to him. He has every blessing that we need. There is nothing we can ever stand in need of but God has it. All blessings come from God; he is the Giver of 'every good gift and every perfect gift'. He has put them all in Christ, and he has given us

Christ. 'All things are yours,' says Paul to the Corinthians. Why? Because 'ye are Christ's'. It is an inevitable piece of logic. It is good for me to draw near to God because when I am near to God I know my sins are forgiven; but when I am far from God I begin to doubt it. I cannot deal with a guilty conscience. I can deal still less with the accusations of other people, or of the devil. It is only when I am near to God in Christ that I know my sins are forgiven. I feel his love, I know I am his child and I enjoy the priceless blessings of peace with God and peace within and peace with others. I am aware of his love and I am given a joy that the world can neither give nor take away.

Anyone who has ever tasted of these things must say that there is nothing comparable to being near to God. Look back across your life. Pick out the most glorious moments in your experience, the moments of supreme peace and joy. Have they not been the times when you have been nearest to God? There is nothing to equal the happiness and joy and peace which result from being near to God. There you are lifted up above your circumstances. You begin to know something of what Paul meant when he said, 'I have learned, in whatsoever state I am, therewith to be content,' 'I know both how to be abased, and I know how to abound.' You are made independent of circumstances and accident and chance, independent of all things. It is good to be near to God because it is the place of salvation, because it is the place where you experience all the blessings. It means that you are immersed in the ocean of God's love and are staying there. Let us adopt this man's resolve to keep near to God.

But in addition to all this, it is also a place of safety. 'But it is good for me to draw near to God: I have put my trust in the Lord God.' We need this, too. As we look into the unknown future we do not know what awaits us. Anything may happen. And if there is one thing we, and the whole world, crave for at this moment, it is security and safety. We have been let down so often; we have even let ourselves down. The thoughtful person asks, 'Where can I repose my trust? On what can I bank with an absolute sense of safety?' And there is still only one answer. It is God. It is good for me to draw near to God; I have put my trust in this Lord God, this Jehovah, this covenant-keeping God.

The Psalms, of course, constantly emphasize this. You find it also in the book of Proverbs. 'The name of the Lord is a strong tower: the righteous runneth into it, and is safe' (Proverbs 18:10). Someone is outside in the world and the enemy begins to attack him. He cannot deal with him; he does not know what to do; he is alarmed and terrified. Then he runs into the strong tower, the name of the Lord, this Lord Jehovah. The enemy cannot get in there. In the arms of God, these almighty arms, he is safe. Yes, says the apostle John, 'we know that we are of God, and the whole world lieth in the evil one,' and 'that evil one cannot touch us' (see 1 John 5:19, 18). Why not? Because we are in Christ, we are in God. We are perfectly safe there. Let me quote again one of the grandest things the apostle Paul ever said: 'I am persuaded [he is certain], that neither death, nor life, nor angels, nor principalities, nor powers, nor things present, nor things to come, nor height, nor depth, nor any other creature, shall be able to separate us from the love of God, which is in Christ Jesus our Lord' (Romans 8:38, 39). Safe in the arms of Jesus. If you are there, though hell be let loose it cannot touch you. Nothing can harm those who are in the safe keeping of their covenant-keeping God.

The last thing the Psalmist mentions is again very wonderful. Let me just note it. 'It is good for me to draw near to God: I have put my trust in the Lord God, that I may declare all thy works.' Now this is a very vital addition. This is the point at which we should all arrive. His final reason for determining to keep near to God is in order that he might glorify God, in order that he might declare all his works. I imagine his argument was something like this: If I keep near to God I shall be blessed, I shall experience his salvation, I shall have this great and marvellous sense of security. And of course that will immediately lead me to praise God and to magnify God and to glorify God before others. I am going to keep near to God in order that I may always praise him, and as I praise God I will be testifying about him to others. That is a point at which we must all arrive.

You remember that the first question in the Shorter

Catechism of the Westminster Confession of Faith is 'What is the chief end of man?' And the answer is that, 'Man's chief end is to glorify God, and to enjoy him for ever.' Now the Psalmist puts it the other way round. He puts enjoyment first only because he is dealing with the matter experimentally. He had been deeply unhappy himself, so he comes down to our own level and he says: Keep near to God and you will be happy, you will enjoy God and you will glorify him. These two things must always go together. 'Man's chief end is to glorify God, and to enjoy him for ever.' Yes, says this man, I am going to keep near to God in order that I may glorify him as well as enjoy him. He is the great Lord God Almighty, and the human tragedy and the tragedy of the world and of history is that the world does not know that. But my business is to tell people about him. I will do so in my life, I will do so with my lips. The whole of my life shall be to the glory of God; and I cannot glorify God unless I am near to him and experiencing him. But as I do so I shall reflect his life.

Thus we have looked at this man's resolve, and we have looked at his reasons for making it. May I remind you, briefly, how all this is to be done? It is not enough to say, Keep near to God, and if you do so these things will happen. How do I keep near to God? We must get down to the practical level. You and I as Christians know that we can always draw near to God in Jesus Christ. We need not scale the heights or descend to the depths. 'The word is nigh thee, even in thy mouth, and in thy heart: . . . that if thou shalt confess with thy mouth the Lord Jesus, and shalt believe in thine heart that God hath raised him from the dead, thou shalt be saved' (Romans 10:8, 9). We need not worry about this, because, if we are Christians at all, we know that, however much we may have sinned, however much wrong we may have done to others and to ourselves, if at this moment we come to God and confess our sins, admitting that we cannot undo them or save ourselves, and trusting entirely in the Son of God and what he has done on our behalf, by his life of obedience and his sacrificial saving death, we are accepted of God, we are reconciled to God, we are in communion with God. That is the way. Yes, but remember to keep near to God. That is this man's resolve. How are we to do it? First of all by a life of prayer. I must insist upon this. If I believe all I have been saying, then I believe that I can talk to God. If I realize truly who he is, I shall want to talk to him. The person who really keeps near to God is the person who is always talking to God. We must resolve to do this; we must decide that we will not allow the world to control us any longer, but that we are going to control it, and our time, and our energy and everything else.

Then in addition to prayer, there is Bible reading. In this book God speaks to you. Therefore read and study the Scriptures.

Next comes public worship. It was when he went into the sanctuary of God that this man found peace and rest for his soul. And we have often had the same experience. If we want to keep near to God, we must not only pray in private, but also with others, we must not only read and study the Word in private, but also come and do so with others. We help one another, we bear one another's burdens.

Then there is meditation and taking time to think. Throw the newspaper on one side and think about God and about your soul and about all these things. We do not talk enough to ourselves. We must tell ourselves that we are in his presence, that we are his children, that Christ has died for us and that he has reconciled us to God. We must practise the presence of God, and realize it, we must talk to him, and spend our days with him. That is the method. To draw near to God means to seek him, and never to allow ourselves any peace or rest until we know that our sins are forgiven, until we know God, until we know the love of God, until we are conscious that when we pray he is ready to listen.

The final thing, of course, is obedience, because if we disobey him we break contact. Sin always means a breaking of the connection, it means going far away from God. So the two rules are, to seek God and then to obey him. And if we should sin, so breaking the contact and communion, we immediately re-establish it by confessing our sins, knowing that 'the blood of Jesus Christ his Son' cleanses us from all unrighteousness.

God grant that as we face the future this may be our heartfelt resolve – 'For me, nearness to God is good for me.' May we know him and dwell with him and spend the remainder of our days really basking in the sunshine of his face and enjoying blessed fellowship with him.

Confess in detail

Bad thoughts

Bad language or said
   something wrong

harbored bad thoughts
   about people

John fletcher

1. Was I idle & lazy?
2. Did I let my mind wander?
3. Have I made the most of my time?
4. Did I do any thing to deny
   myself?
5. Did my life bring glory to
   Christ?
6. Did I 'guard my tongue?